BEATING TIME

Beating Time

A Musician's Memoir

HARRY ELLIS
DICKSON

NORTHEASTERN UNIVERSITY PRESS
Boston

Northeastern University Press

Library of Congress Cataloging-in-Publication Data

Dickson, Harry Ellis.
Beating time : a musician's memoir / Harry Ellis Dickson.
p.   cm.
Includes index.
ISBN 1-55553-229-2 (acid-free paper)
1. Dickson, Harry Ellis. 2. Violinists—United States—Biography.
I. Title.
ML418.D42A3   1995
787.2'092—dc20
[B]   94-39320

Designed by Diane Levy

Composed in Weiss by Graphic Composition, Athens, Georgia. Printed and
bound by Maple Press, York, Pennsylvania. The paper is Sebago Antique, an
acid-free stock.

MANUFACTURED IN THE UNITED STATES OF AMERICA
99   98   97   96   95   5   4   3   2

To Kitty and Jinny

Contents

Contents

Illustrations

Illustrations

With Dukakis, Joan Kennedy, and John Williams
Harry Ellis Dickson Park
A Youth Concerts party
With Natalie Jacobson and Chet Curtis
Conducting a matinee performance

Foreword

~ In the rush of events, so much is forgotten . . . so many marvelous people and their fascinating stories are put aside and consigned to oblivion that we need to applaud the presence of a writer with a keen memory and sharp pen who seeks to put this situation right.

With a fanfare and a flourish we can acknowledge Harry Ellis Dickson for doing just that. Harry's gifts for anecdote, reminiscence, and just plain great storytelling all combine to give vibrance to Boston's ever-bustling musical life, past and present.

There is no greater musical historian on the current cultural scene than Harry. As a conductor, violinist, author, and beloved personality, he's been not simply a witness to the last fifty years of music making in Boston, but a powerful, creative force in it. He's worked with all the major conductors, soloists, singers, and entertainers during one of music's richest periods, and he brings it all to life in *Beating Time*.

It's true: Harry is wonderful! He is a master musician with an elephant's memory and he loves to recall everything that's printable. For the unprintable parts, dear reader, take him to dinner—he's the best after-dinner speaker since the late George Jessel!

Foreword

Personally, I am enormously indebted to Harry for years of support and encouragement during my tenure as conductor of the Boston Pops Orchestra, and I know that all readers of this book will also be in his debt after imbibing the joys contained herein. American musical life is so much richer for Harry's long and lustrous presence in it. Along with all those who love him I look forward to his continuing to "beat time" for many years to come.

JOHN WILLIAMS

Acknowledgments

↶ My friend Neil Savage, who helped in putting this book together (mostly from my memories), is a self-confessed Philistine in music. Or at least he was when we started. "No, Neil, Beethoven did not write an *Erotica* Symphony." He knows so much more now. I acknowledge my great debt to him for his invaluable help, his optimism, and his encouragement.

To my good friends the Bookspans, Jan and Marty, who are to music what wine is to good living, I am indebted. It was Jan, ever creative, who presented me with the title of this book, for which I am ever grateful. And thanks so very much to Marty for his helpful comments and factual corrections.

To Bridget Carr, the extremely capable archivist of the Boston Symphony Orchestra, my sincere thanks and appreciation. She is a dear.

To dear Charlotte Kaufman, for her sunny optimism, misplaced belief in me, and invaluable help in reading and correcting the manuscript—and for so much more—I am forever grateful.

To Bill Frohlich, for encouraging me and forcing me to go through with it, I do owe a great deal.

HED

Preface: "You Look Marvelous!"

 I have been through four ages in my life: childhood, youth, middle age, and "you look marvelous!" Eleven years ago, at age seventy-five, it suddenly occurred to me that I was an old man, a thought I had subconsciously hidden from myself. Now that I am eighty-six, I find there are a few advantages to being an octogenarian. One of them is being respected just for your age. People my age are supposed to have wisdom and a deep understanding of the meaning of life. Frankly, I'm still trying to figure out what it's all about!

Since I have lived so long—longer than most of the people I knew—I have a desire to tell about my life; how it was and is. I have never considered myself especially talented, yet I have always had an insatiable ambition and a most vivid imagination. I imagined myself performing in public and have spent a lifetime doing just that. I imagined myself playing in the Boston Symphony Orchestra and did, for forty-nine years. I imagined myself conducting orchestras and have—and still do! I imagined myself being honored and have been, with twelve honorary degrees, a Chevalier dans l'Ordre des Arts et des Lettres from the govern-

Preface

ment of France, numerous citations, and a park just behind Symphony Hall dedicated in my honor by the city of Boston.

The city of Cambridge, Massachusetts, has seen fit to memorialize some of its distinguished citizens by placing a plaque on the house where each was born or lived. Among those so honored have been the celebrated poets Henry Wadsworth Longfellow and James Russell Lowell; the eminent jurist Oliver Wendell Holmes; and a fiddler, Harry Ellis Dickson. I am grateful.

This is not a book about music or music appreciation—I leave those subjects to scholars, historians, and musicologists. It is merely the chronicle of a long life, a life that has spanned most of this century: reminiscences and anecdotes, some related to music, others not; my own thoughts, experiences, and opinions, some serious, others cynical, and some facetious. There has been very little research; I have written mostly from memory.

Prelude

↶ On Sunday evening, December 19, 1993—five weeks after my eighty-fifth birthday—I left Boston's Logan Airport on an Aer Lingus flight to Dublin. From there I was driven the one hundred miles through a still amazingly green countryside to Belfast, in Northern Ireland. The purpose of my travel was that of much of my life—music. I was to conduct the Ulster Orchestra in a series of "Christmas Pops, Boston Style" concerts, one at the Guildhall in the city of Derry and three at Ulster Hall, Belfast. The trip had been arranged by Boston-Ireland Ventures, a group of business-men dedicated to improving economic opportunity for the people of Northern Ireland.

Belfast is gloomy in the winter. There is hardly any sun and the days are short. Daylight does not begin until almost nine o'clock and it is already quite dark by four-thirty.

I had what were perhaps normal misgivings about going to a "strife-torn" country. I had read about shootings, riots, and bomb-ings in the streets; about religious prejudice and general instabil-ity. An occasional police van drove by. One was stationed at a crossroad attended by a couple of armed patrolmen, and the fa-cade of the Hotel Europa was being restored after a recent bomb

Prelude

attack. But these were the only signs of trouble. Stores were filled with Christmas shoppers; people greeted each other on the street. I looked for telltale signs of who was a Protestant and who was a Catholic, but could see none.

The Ulster Orchestra is a well-run organization, with fine professional musicians and a dedicated staff. I had two full rehearsals with them on Tuesday, and on Wednesday we drove the seventy miles to Derry. Wherever I go to conduct orchestras, I find a kinship among my fellow musicians. After ten minutes of rehearsal there is a feeling of complete fellowship.

The highlight of the concert for me was conducting the orchestra, accompanied by the two cathedral choirs, one Protestant and one Catholic, in a spirited sing-along of "Let There Be Peace on Earth." As I turned to the audience, they were all standing and singing, many with tears in their eyes.

Perhaps one day, peace!

1

Downbeat

❧ By 1905 the Russian Empire was coming to an end. The imperial armies of Czar Nicholas II had been repeatedly defeated by the Japanese on land, and the imperial navy decisively routed at sea. Riots and strikes broke out throughout the industrial heart of Russia. My father was eighteen years old at the time, ripe for induction into the czar's army, where young Jews were considered especially fine cannon fodder. He lived in the town of Kozeletz, a sort of county seat not far from Kiev, in the Ukraine. He had gone to Kiev to learn the tailoring trade, and when he returned he married my mother, four years older than he. The two of them left Kozeletz to take the long journey to America, to Cambridge, Massachusetts.

Why Cambridge? Not by chance. The first to arrive there had been Max Kramer, a cousin of mine, who then made it his business to import the entire family. In Cambridge lived a great clan of relatives. There were Duchins, Marcuses, Kramers, Bennetts, Rosenbergs, Siegals, and Dicksons.

As a matter of fact my name, Dickson, is a fraud. I am a Duchin. (The pianist Eddie Duchin was a cousin of mine.) That family name, though good enough for me, was changed before my birth

Beating Time

to Dickson. As the story goes, my grandfather so disliked his nefarious cousin Duchin, a reputed drunkard and wife beater, that he changed his name to Dickson when he arrived in America. I will be the last with the Dickson name, since I have no male Dickson relatives; my daughters and all my female cousins are married and have different surnames.

Although my birth certificate lists my mother's maiden name as Mirkin, which it was in Russia, her family changed their name to Marcus in America. A change of name was quite common among Russian immigrants. I think it was because of a fear that even in America one might not escape the long arm of the czar's police.

The house to which the city of Cambridge affixed the plaque in my honor is a three-decker, 254 Western Avenue. At various times our small apartment, or "flat" as it was called, housed my mother and father, my two sisters, me, an aunt and uncle, and grandparents. How, I don't know! I was born there, in the back bedroom, the second of three children, on Friday, November 13, 1908.

That year the Republican party nominated William Howard Taft as its presidential candidate; the Socialist party's nominee was a great hero of my father's, Eugene V. Debs. The University of Pennsylvania won the national football championship with a record of eleven wins, no losses, and one tie. The city of Boston banned the novel *Three Weeks* by Elinor Glynn; smoking by women was forbidden in New York City; Isadora Duncan danced scenes from Gluck's *Iphigénie en Aulide*; the famous impresario and father of the American Dance Hall, Tony Pastor, died; and Mischa Elman, the great violin virtuoso, made his American debut at Carnegie Hall.

When my parents arrived in America they did not speak English. My father seemed to have learned the language quickly, while Mama always spoke in a mixture of Yiddish and pidgin English. All my life I conversed with her in Yiddish and spoke only English with my father. In the years I traveled with the Boston Symphony Orchestra, the letters my mother insisted on receiving were all written in Yiddish. I am told that I hardly spoke English myself until I entered kindergarten at age four years and ten months.

My father opened a small tailor shop in our neighborhood in Cambridge and earned enough money to support us. Although we may have been considered poor, we dressed well and were never hungry. In our house it was a sin not to eat. I remember Mama's constant admonition: "Ess, ess, mein kind" (Eat, eat, my child).

In our home physical punishment was a no-no. "Only the *goyim* beat their children," my mother used to say. She actually pushed open the door of an Italian neighbor's house one day where a woman was beating her child, tore a strap out of the woman's hand, and warned her that she would call the police if it happened again. My mother, strong and fearless, so frightened the woman that the beatings stopped.

Our neighborhood was made up of immigrant Jews and blacks, and we knew little about prejudice as a fact of life. One of my close friends was a black boy named Willie who lived across the street. We played together and visited each other's homes. My second-grade teacher was a black woman whom I adored. I can even remember her name after all these years—Miss Moran.

There were the usual rowdies in the street. Bums, we used to call them. They occasionally made disparaging remarks as bearded Jews passed by. One day my paternal grandfather questioned my father about the law of self-protection in this country.

Beating Time

My grandfather was a tall, powerful man who had been a blacksmith in the old country.

"Can I fight back?" he asked. "Only if he touches you first," my father answered. Some time later, as my grandfather was walking home from the synagogue, one of those bums took it upon himself to harass him by yanking his beard, at which point my grandfather stepped on the culprit's foot and punched him in the face, breaking his jaw and toe. After that the watchword in the neighborhood was, "Leave the old man Dickson alone."

My maternal grandfather was very different. He was small in stature, kind, gentle, lovable. I adored him. He had been a grain merchant in Russia, and it was said of him that if he met anyone who owed him money, he would ask for it and then add, "If you don't have it now, you can pay me later."

After our family had moved out of our old neighborhood, I would return every Friday afternoon to spend the Sabbath with him and my two uncles and aunts. On Saturday morning my grandfather would leave early for the synagogue, and I would join him later. One morning on his way, he spotted a fifty-cent piece on the ground. A half dollar was the better part of many a man's hourly wage in those days. Here was a temptation. It must be remembered that an Orthodox Jew cannot handle money on the Sabbath, not even carry it in his pocket.

My grandfather looked at the coin, then spread dirt over it with his foot. On the way back from services he was careful to lead me to the spot where the coin was buried. Well aware that an Orthodox Jew may not advise anyone to do something sacrilegious, he alluded mysteriously to "buried treasure," never advising me to dig it up. As he walked on ahead, I, of course, dug up the coin and put it in my pocket. "Did you find it?" he asked when I caught up with

Downbeat

him. I nodded and he said, "Good!" To the day he died nothing was said about it. I wish I could say that I still had that fifty-cent piece!

Shortly before my beloved grandfather died, I visited him in the hospital. His mind was gone, and even when I told him who I was, he did not recognize me. He asked, "Do you know my grandson?" and then proceeded to praise me while the tears rolled down my cheeks.

My father was a socialist, a member of the Arbiter Ring, the Jewish Socialist Workmen's Circle. He had a fine singing voice, and when the high holidays came and the congregation was seeking a cantor, Eliahu—my father's Hebrew name, which was anglicized to Ellis—was given the task of auditioning the applicants, even though he was not a religious man. Quite handsome, my father acted in amateur theatrical groups, which performed works by Yiddish playwrights such as Shalom Aleichem and Sholem Asch, and the composer Joseph Rumshinsky. He was also instrumental in the formation of a credit union where immigrants—Irish, Italian, Jewish—could put their money to earn a little interest, and to borrow some to go into business or for other good reasons. My father was secretary-treasurer of the credit union and taught himself the necessary bookkeeping.

We had a family organization proudly called the Dickson Descendants, which held regular meetings on a rotating basis in the homes of different relatives. Our family was large, and there were a fair number of "characters" among us. My father, being the oldest, was president of the Descendants and the formality of the meetings required that he be addressed as either Brother President or Uncle President.

There was always a place in the agenda where my father would

Beating Time

announce, "Good and welfare," whatever that meant. Aunt Bessie, who seemed always to be sick, would ask, "Can we talk about sick benefits?" My father would say to his sister, "Bessie, you are out of order!"

Occasionally there were some embarrassing moments such as when Uncle Harry, the most tactless person I have ever known, announced, "My wife has become cold to me." His wife, my aunt Rose, was furious! My father, wanting to keep up the suspense, asked, "When did you notice this?"—to which Uncle Harry answered, "About three o'clock this morning!" Uncle Harry was the one who, when guests stayed too late, would say to Aunt Rose, "Let's go to bed. Maybe they want to go home."

We put on vaudeville shows at one of the high schools in Dorchester, my family and a few others. My father used to sing, my uncle Percy was the makeup artist, and my aunts danced in a sort of ensemble. In one of the acts I remember, my uncle Percy dressed himself up as a musician, with a wig and a high collar, and pretended to play the fiddle. We arranged it so that I was playing in back of a screen, and Percy just made the motions. My aunt Bessie turned to her sister in amazement and asked, "Where did Percy learn to play the violin?"

Eventually Uncle Harry and my father opened a tailor shop in Cambridge between Harvard and Central squares. My father made women's clothing, Harry made men's. Some of the most distinguished professors at Harvard and MIT would have suits made by Uncle Harry. Uncle Harry was a perfectionist and very proud of his craft. If he made a suit and wasn't satisfied with it, he'd rip it apart and start all over again. A ready-made suit was an aberration for him. "What kind of a rag is that? Look at it! Machine buttonholes!"

Downbeat

In 1916 our family moved to Somerville where my aunt Bessie lived. My mother had become a victim of the Spanish influenza, which was ravaging much of the world at that time. The authorities concluded that it had reached Massachusetts, carried by sailors on one of the ships that docked in Boston. Aunt Bessie prevailed on my father to move to Somerville so that she could help care for my mother. From the fifth grade through high school I belonged to Somerville. Our new flat was directly across from a funeral parlor, and I can remember seeing from my window coffins being piled up on the street.

My father's role in the family tailoring business was not going well. His expertise as a "women's tailor" was beginning to become obsolete in an assembly line economy. A neighbor told him that the Boston Elevated Railway was looking for conductors. My father applied, took the necessary examination, was accepted, and became a streetcar conductor. His run was from Somerville to the North Station in Boston. My older sister and I used to wait for his trolley knowing that we'd get a free ride. When he got to his destination, he would announce in his rich accent: "North Stayshel," and we would laugh hilariously, for the word *stayshel* in Yiddish means a cooking pot.

In my memory of early years in Somerville, Miss Norcross in the sixth grade stands out. Miss Norcross, with whom I had a great deal of difficulty, was a tall, erect woman with white hair. At the time I estimated her age to be about a hundred. She was a strict disciplinarian, and I was an unruly brat whom she excused to others in the class by saying, "We must tolerate Harry because he is the youngest." She was, in retrospect, a wonderful teacher, and if I possess even a smattering of good grammar and proper spelling, it was learned in the sixth grade with Miss Norcross.

Beating Time

Miss Norcross kept me after school a lot until one day my mother came to school and scolded her for keeping me from my Hebrew lessons. I was embarrassed and cringed at my mother's strange English.

Evidently my mother's visit straightened things out between her and Miss Norcross. I stopped going to Hebrew school and eventually had a tutor, Rabbi Kaplan. My parents wanted me not only to learn Hebrew but also to learn to write Yiddish, the language we spoke at home. My grandfather and grandmother and aunts and uncles spoke no English. To this day I can read and write Yiddish.

I was bar mitzvahed at thirteen. My bar mitzvah was an emotional one since I was the oldest grandson of my maternal grandfather. I composed my own speech (usually done for the bar mitzvah boy by the rabbi) and impressed everybody. After my bar mitzvah my attendance at temple was sporadic, although I did attend services with my parents on high holidays. There were no breaks in the services in those days. On Yom Kippur my mother would sit in the synagogue all day long. I would go up to the balcony, where the women were segregated, to talk to her. "Go home and eat something," she would say. She didn't want me to fast; she thought I was too young for that.

At the age of sixteen I felt a spiritual awakening and began going to synagogue every day. The members of the congregation looked at me strangely, wondering why a young man would come to services each day, unless to say the Kaddish (the memorial prayer) for a deceased parent. "Why aren't you saying the Kaddish?" they would ask. When I told them my parents were still alive, they were impressed, if puzzled.

One day I got a translation of the Kaddish and discovered to my amazement that not a word in it referred to the dead. It was a

Downbeat

prayer extolling God. I remember talking to my father about it and he said, "It's nonsense. You don't have to say it for me." It was then that I stopped going to services every day.

Somerville High School produced some well-known athletes in the days when I was a student there, especially baseball players. Danny MacFayden pitched for seventeen years in the big leagues. Haskell Billings was another major-league pitcher from Somerville High. But the best known of my classmates was James "Shanty" (we called him "Gimpy") Hogan, a fine catcher who spent thirteen years in the majors with a lifetime batting average of .295. The alumnus of Somerville High to achieve the greatest athletic fame before my time was Pie Traynor, the great third baseman of the Pittsburgh Pirates.

I didn't participate in sports, but I was in awe of athletes. Still, I managed to earn a letter—by playing the cymbals and bass drum in the high school band. We played at all the games. I remember one baseball game when a batter for the opposing team accused me of flashing my cymbals in his eyes and threatened me with his bat.

Mr. Maynard, the band supervisor, was terribly nearsighted, almost blind. I was something of a rascal and would switch instruments at rehearsals. He'd suddenly stop and say, "There's something wrong in the horn section. Is that you, Dickson?" I'd run back to the bass drum and cymbals, where I belonged.

We used to practice marching up and down in front of the high school, with Mr. Maynard marching alongside us. I would make a signal for the band to turn right and march down the street and poor Mr. Maynard would keep going—straight ahead!

2

"Vat kind note is dis?"

~ My career in music began when I was about six and a half. My older sister, Rebecca (now called Ruth), who was then eight, was taking violin lessons from Mr. Sugarman, the neighborhood klezmer. A klezmer was a musician who played at bar mitzvahs and weddings and gave lessons. Mr. Sugarman came to our house about once a week to torture my sister, who had absolutely no talent. For some reason, I was allowed to sit in. I was soon surreptitiously taking my sister's violin out of its case and trying it on my own. At one of her lessons, Mr. Sugarman was asking Rebecca the names of different notes and their values. I still remember the questions. Mr. Sugarman would point to a note and ask: "And vat kind note is dis?"—to which my sister had no answer. I would pipe up: "That's F sharp." "And vat kind note is dis?" Sugarman would persist, and Rebecca wouldn't have a clue, so I would answer for her: "That's a D."

I don't remember all the details, but subsequently the violin was taken away from my sister and given to me with the advice of Mr. Sugarman, who offered to teach me for nothing.

To say I was in love with the violin and the sound I thought it would produce is an understatement. We had a recording that I

11

Beating Time

kept playing over and over again on our Victrola: Mischa Elman playing Massenet's Elegy. I was completely mesmerized by that beautiful sound, which I longed to be able to reproduce.

I practiced a great deal. I was ambitious. I wanted to be better than the other kids, especially the Teitelbaum boys, who lived next door. (Not very hard. They were pretty bad.) It was competitive among the parents of the kids taking violin lessons, and I was held up as sort of an example, especially by the Teitelbaums.

In retrospect, I do not believe I was as talented as I was ambitious. I was not a musical genius, but my imagination carried me to the greatest heights. While I practiced I was transported to the stages of every concert hall in the world. I remember constantly trying to out-do my own practicing record. One day at the age of twelve I practiced an entire day. My mother kept admonishing me, "It's enough already!" and finally took the violin from my hands.

Mr. McVey, the music teacher at Somerville High, was a knowledgeable musician, able to transmit his own enthusiasm to his students, and he quickly influenced my life. We had a good orchestra at Somerville High School, trained by Mr. McVey, who made me concertmaster. We played all the standard classics. The first time I ever heard Weber's *Freischutz* Overture was at Somerville High. I also vividly remember the *Pastoral* Symphony of Beethoven and Mr. McVey's explanation of the scherzo, in which the oboe seems to enter a beat late, which was, according to Mr. McVey, Beethoven's description of a confused country musician.

The supervisor of music for the Somerville school system at that time was Russell Ames Cook. He and his wife, Clara, became very close to my family and me over the years. One day Russell Cook asked if anyone would be interested in playing in his Pea-

"Vat kind note is dis?"

body House Orchestra, the Peabody House being a settlement house in the West End of Boston. Of course I was, and I attended weekly rehearsals for a number of years.

A few of my young colleagues in that orchestra later became professionals, among them the violinists Robert Gomberg and his sister Celia. Bobby later played in the Philadelphia Orchestra, and Celia was an internationally known soloist.

Bobby Gomberg was thirteen and I was about fourteen at the time. Even though we were youngsters, we always had an eye out for making money. He came from a poor family and so did I. At rehearsals Bobby sat next to me. His first question was always "How's business?" Both of us were often engaged to play at various functions such as ladies' clubs and the Ford Hall Forum.

At age fourteen, while still in high school, I found myself on the B. F. Keith vaudeville circuit leading a twelve-piece orchestra. The players were recruited from the high school orchestra by a Catholic priest, Father Hagen. We were a vaudeville act with a lady singer, Grace Hushen and Her Melody Boys, and we played in different theaters throughout New England, mostly in the summer, during school vacations. Occasionally we had permission to leave school early to play a matinee. Miss Hushen had a manager, Charlie Ross, who booked us into the vaudeville houses around Boston. There were vaudeville houses everywhere, and we played at most of them: the Keith Memorial, the Lancaster at North Station, the Gordon Central Square in Cambridge, and numerous others. I don't remember what we were paid, but to me it was a fortune.

Grace Hushen, uneducated, uncultured, but with a good voice, was the most beautiful woman I had ever known, and at fourteen

Beating Time

I was madly in love with her. She was probably in her middle thirties, and her motherly concern for me, the youngest of the group, was touching. I was a homesick, immature, underdeveloped kid, and on one of our out-of-town tours I found myself in her hotel room bed, where she offered to comfort me. Nothing happened sexually, but for a long time afterward I worried that she was pregnant. Weren't babies made by lying next to a woman?

We used to rehearse in each other's homes, and I remember one rehearsal in my house (we had a rather large parlor) when we were practicing a new piece. "Let's take it slowly at first," I suggested, but Grace, who knew nothing about music and always insisted on exercising her authority, said, "No! If you play it slow you'll learn it slow!"

At one of our performances at the Gordon Central Square Theater in Cambridge, my entire family was in the audience: parents, grandparents, uncles, aunts, cousins. After my solo performance (a Brahms Hungarian Dance), which was part of the act, the stage was pelted with cascades of flowers.

My "career" with Grace Hushen and Her Melody Boys lasted for a couple of years. Then, with the impending demise of vaudeville, it was over. In retrospect I hated the entire experience musically, but to a young boy, the glamour of being on stage was seductive.

In my senior year of high school our family moved from Somerville to Wayland Street in the Dorchester section of Boston, and I had to commute the very long distance to Somerville High on public transportation. I graduated in June 1925, at sixteen years of age. What to do? In those days Jewish sons became doctors or lawyers, and for a while I considered medicine. I took the examinations for Harvard and passed them. Yet in my heart and mind,

"Vat kind note is dis?"

music was my life. I had begun to practice less and less, until one evening at supper my father remarked that the house seemed empty without "Hershel's fiddle." Then and there my future was determined. I applied, auditioned, and was accepted at the New England Conservatory of Music for the class beginning in September.

3

Studying at the New England
Conservatory

ᕦ The New England Conservatory of Music is the oldest music
school in America. Founded in 1867 by Eben Tourjée, a musical
zealot who established the classroom system of teaching music in
the United States, the New England Conservatory led the way
long before such schools as Eastman, Peabody, Juilliard, and Curtis came into existence.

I knew nothing about violin teachers at the conservatory, and
it was only a chance recommendation that led me to Vaughn
Hamilton, an enthusiastic teacher who, over the years, became a
good friend and mentor. Up to the time I went to the conservatory, I was using a cheap violin. Hamilton got me a better one for
which my father paid four or five hundred dollars—a lot of money
in those days. Hamilton was a member of the Boston Symphony
Orchestra. At that time there was no way of knowing that someday I would occupy his very seat in the orchestra.

Two other pedagogues on the violin faculty were quite eminent:
Eugene Gruenberg, the author of numerous violin studies and exercises, and Harrison Keller, a kindly man who had studied with

Beating Time

the famous Leopold Auer. Even though my teacher was Vaughn Hamilton, I developed a friendly relationship with Keller and occasionally played for him. Keller later became the director of the conservatory.

When I enrolled at the conservatory in 1925, the director was George Whitefield Chadwick, a feisty New England Yankee. Chadwick was a composer of some prestige who had studied in Europe and whose compositions were played by American orchestras, including the Boston Symphony. He presided over the conservatory with fatherly concern, and when I discovered that we had the same birthday, I went to his office to apprise him of that coincidence. He patted my head, said, "That's nice," and dismissed me. Each year on our common birthday, I would knock on his door. "Come in!" he would order. "Oh, it's you, Dickson, it must be our birthday." On one of his last birthdays he was ill and at home, so Cecile Forrest, a fellow student, and I went to his house to play for him. We chose the unaccompanied Sonatina for Two Violins by Arthur Honegger, a piece Chadwick had never heard. He was upstairs in his bedroom, and we played at the foot of the stairs. When we finished we heard a chuckle. "Now," he said, "I know what's worse than a fiddle. Two fiddles!"

There was an established custom in those days for teachers to send their talented students to play for Chadwick. On one of these impromptu occasions I was chosen to play the Nigun from the Baal-shem Suite of Ernest Bloch. After I had finished, Chadwick's comment was "Too Jewish." It was then that I became aware of a certain amount of Yankee anti-Semitism among the establishment figures at the conservatory.

Chadwick occasionally conducted the conservatory orchestra, in which I was concertmaster. During one of Chadwick's own compositions (was it the *Melpomene* Overture?) Larry White, a fine percussionist who later joined the Boston Symphony, mistakenly came in with a loud cymbal crash at the wrong time. Chadwick uttered a loud epithet. A number of weeks later, White had the misfortune of running into Chadwick in the corridor. Chadwick shook his finger at him and screamed, "You son of a bitch, you ruined my piece!"

There were other composers of note at the conservatory at that time including Frederic Converse, Arthur Foote, and Stuart Mason. Two conservatory teachers stand out in my mind: the kindly, goateed Clement Lenom, and the sparkling wit Stuart Mason. Lenom, formerly an oboist with the Boston Symphony, was the solfeggio teacher, and his classes were filled with joyous musical delights and discussions. "What the devil is solfeggio?" I asked when I was told it was part of the curriculum. Later I became convinced of the value of a system for reading music at sight, like reading a book. Lenom taught his classes with great exuberance, and he attracted many who were not even registered as students. It did not matter. "Everyone is welcome," he used to say.

Stuart Mason was my harmony and composition teacher. His classes also were open to everyone. Mason had an infectious, impish exuberance and wit, and even held special classes two nights a week (for which he was not paid) for anyone interested. It was at these classes that I made my first meager attempt at composition; a fantasy on a Hebrew theme my father had taught me, which I later conducted at a conservatory concert, to the delight of my parents.

The ensemble classes at the conservatory were in the charge of Josef Adamowski, a bearded, temperamental, sarcastic Pole. Everyone was afraid of "Uncle Joe," whose outbursts could wither

Beating Time

you. It took a while for him to begin to like me, but once he did, I could do no wrong. He would take me into his confidence in discussing other students.

Uncle Joe sat behind a table, a long stick in his hand, with which he beat time. The corner of the table was well worn from his constant whacking. He had no mercy in his heart, and his favorite pastime was insulting his students. Once we were playing a Mendelssohn trio in which the cellist was a young nun. She was not very experienced, to say the least, and kept getting lost. At one point Uncle Joe spurted out, "Look, Dickson, she looks like angel and plays like devil!"

Adamowski played cello with the Boston Symphony and was also part of the Adamowski Trio, along with his brother Timothy, former concertmaster of the Boston Pops, and his wife, the pianist Antoinette Szumowska. He was rarely pleased. At one time he did compliment the performance of a string quartet in which I played first violin and as a reward took us all out to lunch at a restaurant near the conservatory. When we entered the restaurant, a jukebox was blasting away. Adamowski shouted to the proprietor, "If you do not shut off damn thing, we leave!" There was no more music during lunch.

The conservatory orchestra was regularly conducted by Wallace Goodrich, the dean. He was a typical Back Bay brahmin, stiff, handsome, and completely humorless. His manner of speech always seemed patronizing. His position as dean made him almost untouchable. I don't know much about his musicianship except that he had studied in Germany and was a fine organist whose great love was Richard Wagner. We played a lot of Wagner with the conservatory orchestra. It was during those days that I think I acquired my hatred of Wagner, and later, when I read it, came to

Studying at the New England Conservatory

agree with Mark Twain's observation that "Wagner's music is better than it sounds."

During my conservatory years I was always on the lookout for opportunities to earn money. I found time to play in a Chinese restaurant located across the street from the conservatory. Before the advent of piped-in music, restaurants and the dining rooms of hotels actually had live music. I played at the restaurant every evening with a trio—myself, a pianist, and a cellist.

One summer I played in a trio at a seaside restaurant called Hugo's in Scituate, Massachusetts. It was owned by a jolly, outgoing Hungarian, Hugo Ormo, who loved classical music. I remember Hugo sitting at a table with guests listening to our Mendelssohn when a waitress with a tray of steaming lobsters attempted to cross the dining room. Hugo held up his hand to stop her. There she stood, tray in hand, until the music was over. By that time the lobsters were cold. "You must never interrupt the music," Hugo said. "Now go back and get a fresh tray."

All of this playing came in addition to conservatory classes each day and hours of practice at home. Then a new opportunity opened up for me.

The Movies

I was standing in front of the Beethoven statue in the entrance hall of the conservatory when I was approached by a man who asked if I would be interested in playing at a moviehouse. "Sure I would," I replied, and soon found myself conducting in the pit of one of E. M. Loew's theaters, the beginning of a two-year association with the movie magnate.

Loew was a rough, tough Hungarian immigrant who owned a

Beating Time

string of theaters throughout New England. He had recently added the Day Street Theater in Somerville to his chain, a small neighborhood moviehouse that ran only evening shows. There were eight musicians in the pit, and I was the conductor and violinist. We would begin by playing a short overture, followed by music for the newsreel, a one- or two-reel comedy or short subject, and finally the feature film—all silent, in those days. Each movie came with a cue sheet of recommended music for each episode in the film, with the approximate timing. I would choose the music ahead of time, and during the performance signaled the musical entrances by depressing a foot switch, causing the light on each musician's stand to flicker.

Between the preliminary movies and the feature film there were five or six acts of live vaudeville. After the vaudeville we played for twenty minutes or so into the feature, at which time a pianist would take over. Each Tuesday was "amateur night," when bookers would come to scout new vaudeville acts. On such nights there might be as many as eight or ten acts, most of them pretty awful. I remember dreading Tuesday nights because they were sometimes dangerous. The audience would show their displeasure with a bad act by screaming and shouting insults at the performers, and we musicians were afraid they would take it out on us!

One evening we were actually in mortal danger, not from the audience but from the stage. A group of would-be jugglers were tossing objects to one another, many of them falling to the floor. While we were playing some lively music, I looked up and saw dishes flying in all directions, most of them smashing to the floor in bits. The audience was screaming. When the performers began to throw long-handled knives at one another, and one landed not

Studying at the New England Conservatory

far from me, I felt we had had enough. I motioned my musicians to follow me out of the pit. The manager was furious. I said to him, "You go into the pit! We're not ready to die!"

When E. M. Loew took over the National Theater in Boston's South End, a much larger house than the Day Street, we moved over there for Saturday and Sunday performances. The routine was the same as it had been at the Day Street except that instead of a piano, the grand organ finished the feature picture.

The musicians' room at the National was under the stage, with an entrance to the pit. In this room we developed a warm friendship with the large water rats who inhabited it and who used to peer at us from their perches above the pipes under the ceiling. We even fed them by tossing up scraps of food.

We did four shows a day on Saturday and again on Sunday and would sometimes recognize the same faces sitting in the first few rows throughout all four shows. I remember a girl who seemed to be there in the front row at every performance on both Saturday and Sunday. Flossie was her name, a young, rather attractive French girl who knew some of the musicians. Each time I came into the pit I was greeted with "'Allo, 'Arry."

One night after the show as I was about to leave by the stage door, where my car was parked, Eddie Mandel, our trombone player, shyly and with a grin on his face, said: "Harry, Flossie is waiting for you." (Eddie Mandel was a tremendous trombone player. A simple man, unaware of his own talent, he once played for me the finale of the Mendelssohn Violin Concerto on his trombone, a feat which even to this day I find hard to imagine! Eddie used to make fun of my disdain for jazz. I once told him that when I heard jazz, I thought of naked women carousing. During one of

Beating Time

our performances, when we were playing a jazz piece, Eddie stood up in the pit and asked, "Can you see the naked woman now, Harry?")

It was pouring rain that night, and there, standing by my car, was Flossie. There was no way I could avoid her. "Take me 'ome," she said. I let her get in and drove to her apartment, which wasn't far away. When we got there she wouldn't leave the car. "Come up," she insisted, "otherwise I will not leave ze car."

I was scared stiff. Although I was almost twenty, I was naive when it came to women. Finally I said okay and went around to open the door on her side of the car. As soon as she was out, I raced back to my side, jumped in, and locked all the doors. Flossie, who had started toward her apartment, came running back and stood on the running board as I started the engine. It was still pouring rain, but I opened my window and pushed her into a puddle and sped off. The next afternoon as I walked into the pit for the first performance, there was Flossie in the front row as always. "'Allo, 'Arry!" she greeted me.

It was about that time that silent movies were coming to an end. The first "talking pictures" were recorded in Vitaphone, a complicated system of synchronizing phonograph records to the action on the screen. One day it was announced at the National Theater that a talking picture would be shown on a certain evening. When the night came, all of us musicians assembled in a box seat section after the vaudeville acts. We were joined by E. M. Loew himself to witness this new phenomenon, a movie adaptation of Victor Hugo's *Les Misérables*. Well into the movie came a scene where Jean Valjean, having been convicted, was being sentenced by the judge.

"Jean Valjean," the judge solemnly intoned, "I sentence you to

twenty years at hard labor. What have you to say?" . . . *uhh* . . .
"What have you to say?" . . . *uhh* . . . "What have you to say?" . . .
uhh . . . With the needle stuck, the audience went wild with
screaming and catcalls. The judge was still asking Jean Valjean
what he thought of his sentence while the picture showed the
poor fellow already serving his time, pounding rocks!

Loew, sitting next to me, was livid! He left the box and ran back
to the projection room; I tailed after him. The operator, whose
job it was to see that the sound track on the record coincided with
the action on the screen, looked helpless and confused. When
Loew shouted, "Do something!" the poor man picked up the stuck
needle and put it back to the beginning of the record. Now picture
and dialogue were hopelessly confused. The needle became stuck
again when it came to "What have you to say?" . . . *uhh* . . .

We musicians were relieved. Talking pictures will never succeed, we concluded. But of course we were wrong, and they eventually drove musicians out of the movie theater business.

The primary goal in life for E. M. Loew was the acquisition of
money and power (although he did take care of his relatives,
bringing many over from Hungary). He and I got along reason-
ably well, despite many arguments. My association with E. M.
Loew came to an end when he asked me to stay on as a conductor
at a new theater he had opened in Pawtucket, Rhode Island. I had
conducted the opening there, but a week in Pawtucket was
enough for me. I refused his offer; my studies at the conservatory
were more important to me than the money he offered, which was
very good for those days—sixty-five dollars a week.

"I offer you good money," Loew said, "and all you think of is
your 'opuses'!"

"Mr. Loew," I replied, "if I get to be your age" (I was all of nine-

Beating Time

teen at the time) "and money means as much to me as it does to you, I'll be sorry I lived so long."

"Oh," he said, "you're a crazy musician!" As it turned out, E. M. Loew lived a long time, getting richer and acquiring more and more moviehouses.

Summer in New Hampshire

In the late 1920s, I took a summer job playing at Gray's Inn, a small, swank hotel in Jackson, New Hampshire. Many of the hotels in the White Mountains were restricted, catering mostly to elderly white Protestants. We had a trio (piano, violin, and cello) and played a short concert each afternoon and evening before lunch and dinner. On Wednesday and Saturday nights we added a drummer and saxophone and played for dancing.

The three summers I spent at this idyllic spot were among the happiest of my life. The food was sumptuous; there was tennis and golf and plenty of time for practicing. And I think we were paid quite well.

The owner of the hotel, Colonel Gray (I don't know where he got his title), was a tall, ramrod straight, crusty New England Yankee. We became good friends, and occasionally he invited me to sit with him and his friends at dinner. When, in the fall of 1931, I was preparing to go to Germany to study, I wrote him expressing my sorrow about not returning the following summer. Colonel Gray wrote me a complimentary letter, praising me and my music and asking me to recommend a trio for the following summer. A postscript to his letter read: "Prefer not to have Jewish musicians."

I showed the letter to my father. Livid, he practically dictated my reply:

Studying at the New England Conservatory

Dear Colonel Gray:
If you can possibly overlook their backgrounds, I would like to suggest to you the following musicians: Jascha Heifetz, violin; Artur Rubinstein, piano; and Gregor Piatigorsky, cello.

I never received a reply. I doubt if Colonel Gray had ever heard of any of them!

Back to School

At the commencement program of my class, the class of 1929, I was chosen to be the soloist in the first movement of the Wieniawski D Minor Violin Concerto. Several of my classmates in that orchestra later joined the Boston Symphony.

In those days the New England Conservatory did not issue degrees. That came years later. At the end of four years one received an instrument diploma. Another year earned a so-called Artist Diploma, so I was advised to stay on. This meant another graduation and another solo appearance with the orchestra at the June 1930 graduation exercises. This time, with Wallace Goodrich again conducting, I played the Saint-Saëns Introduction and Rondo Capriccioso. Although I had graduated, I was invited to come back the following year to continue my role as concertmaster of the orchestra, which I did until leaving for Europe in 1931.

4

Berlin, 1931–1933

❧ I marvel at how we have progressed in music education in the United States during the past sixty-five years. Today students from all over the world flock to this country to study at our own music schools and conservatories.

In the 1930s it was fashionable, almost necessary, for American musicians to study abroad, and Berlin was the center of the world's musical activity. Paris, Vienna, London, each had a thriving musical life, but Berlin had the greatest concentration of teachers, performers, and composers, as well as two symphony orchestras and two opera companies, all supported by the government.

During my last year at the New England Conservatory, Vaughn Hamilton suggested that I go to Europe to continue my studies. Some of my friends from the conservatory were already there. I had a talk with Louis Krasner, himself a graduate of the conservatory, who had studied in Europe for many years. Krasner, who is still alive and in his nineties, was a well-known violinist who played the first performance of the Berg Violin Concerto, which had been written for him. He agreed that I should go to Berlin and recommended that I study with Max Rostal, the assistant to the famous violin pedagogue Carl Flesch. Krasner thought that I would do better with Rostal, a younger man and much easier to approach, than with Flesch. Both were well-known teachers.

My parents were not happy about my leaving, especially my mother. She was terribly worried about it, but realized that it was important for my career. I was able to finance my trip to Berlin and my lessons with Rostal from the money I had earned playing, money that my sister Rebecca kept in a bank account for me.

On December 16, 1931, I left for Berlin on the Cunard liner S.S. *Scythia* from East Boston, sailing at midnight directly to Liverpool. The night before I had played with the conservatory orchestra, the Chausson *Poème*, and there had been a party after the concert. I was presented with a "bon voyage" gift, a silver cigarette case (everyone smoked in those days). Many of my orchestra colleagues were at the dock, some with their instruments serenading me as I waved good-bye from the upper deck.

The voyage took eight days. I practiced a lot, but managed to spend some time with a pretty Irish girl (whose name I don't remember), who was returning to Ireland.

When I arrived in Liverpool I went aboard a smaller boat for the nighttime crossing of the English Channel to Holland. It was a rough crossing, and I arrived very sick. I was met by someone from the steamship company who remarked on how bad I looked. Almost immediately I boarded a train for Berlin, where I was met by my friend and fellow violinist Royal Johnson.

Johnson, who later played in the Chicago Symphony, had studied at the New England Conservatory and had been in Berlin for about a year as a student of Rostal. Royal was a happy-go-lucky, irresponsible guy. I had to remind him to write to the lady in Boston who had helped arrange for his stay in Germany over a year

Berlin, 1931–1933

earlier. He immediately sent her a card: "Arrived safely. Everything fine." Royal arranged for me to rent a room in the same house where he lived, on Barbarossastrasse, owned by the elderly Fraulein Winkler.

The next day I telephoned Max Rostal, who spoke a bit of English, and told him who I was. He informed me that he had already heard about me from Louis Krasner and asked me to come to his house, in a suburb of Berlin accessible by train. Fraulein Winkler gave me directions as best she could, but it was a difficult journey, since I hardly spoke German at the time and had to use sign language. I finally found Rostal's house and played for him. He said, "Fine, I will take you," and I began my weekly lessons at his home.

Shortly after my arrival in Berlin, I telephoned Rachelle Shubow, an acquaintance of mine from Boston (her brother was our family dentist) who was studying piano in Berlin. Rachelle was a motherly do-gooder to whom everyone came for advice. She had absolutely no talent but took lessons with the great Artur Schnabel and practiced ten hours a day. Why Schnabel accepted her as a student was a mystery, except that he liked money and was kind.

"Come on over," Rachelle said, "I'm having a party tomorrow evening for some American friends." The party was at her small apartment, and her friends turned out to be mostly medical students who had flunked out of American medical colleges but were able to get into German schools.

One of the girls at Rachelle's party was Jane Goldberg, the daughter of a woman Rachelle had met on the boat over from America. Jane was from New Rochelle, New York. She was beautiful—tall and slender, with wistful, sad eyes. My teachers in Boston

Beating Time

had warned me about getting seriously involved with a girl. My first priority, they said, was to study and practice without distractions. "Don't get entangled, and don't fall in love," they warned.

That advice, as it turned out, I did not follow. I was smitten with Jane. I called her the next night and we went to a movie. Later, I tried hard to minimize our relationship and tried to treat her with a kind of studied nonchalance. I even refused an invitation to spend Christmas vacation with her and her mother in Davos, Switzerland. Jane had a strange background. She had been adopted as an infant by Mabel and Henry Goldberg, a well-to-do childless couple in New Rochelle. Mabel was a completely unconventional, well-educated, kooky radical who was of the opinion that American children should have a European education. She deposited Jane, at age nine, with a French family at Le Puy du Dome, in central France. There Jane went to school until she was fourteen, all that time, of course, learning French and adapting to the French ways of life. She was then yanked out of the French school by her mother and deposited in a school in Frankfurt, the Odenwald Schule. It was a school of new, radical ideas of pedagogy under the direction of a distinguished educator, Paul Geheeb. Jane spent about four years there and left with the equivalency of a high school education, for no diplomas were given at the Odenwald Schule.

When I first met Jane (she was nineteen, I was twenty-three), she was employed at the Spandau Institute for Retarded Children as a social worker. The institute was on the grounds of the infamous Spandau Prison, where Rudolf Hess was to be incarcerated for many years until his death. I visited Jane once at Spandau—about an hour's train ride from Berlin—and vowed never to go there again, it was so depressing. I couldn't understand her willingness to devote herself to those unfortunate children, most of them of noble birth.

Jane spoke perfect French and German, yet I detected a certain hesitancy in her English. There were certain words that she simply did not know. She was completely ignorant of American profanity, and after we were married, I am ashamed to admit, I assigned myself the task of educating her in that art, except that I purposely gave her wrong words and wrong meanings. Jane asked me once what was the slang word for *penis*. I told her the word was *prop*. For years afterward, any time Jane saw or heard the word *prop* she blushed.

After a few months studying with Max Rostal as a private pupil, I told him I was running out of money. He offered to try to get me admitted to the Hochschule für Musik, the Academy of Music. There was no tuition at the academy, and if accepted I would be able to continue my lessons with Rostal, who was a professor there, free of charge.

My audition at the Hochschule was mercifully short. The audition board consisted of George Schoeneman, the director; Carl Flesch; and the renowned cellist Emanuel Feuermann. I had to play part of a Mozart concerto, and then part of the Beethoven Violin Concerto. I was immediately accepted. Feuermann was a bit of a joker. He was writing down what I played and asked, "Mozart in D major?" I said, "Nein, A major." "Thank you," he replied sarcastically.

As a student, I was issued a "student passport" allowing me to get tickets to the opera, theaters, and moviehouses for twenty pfennigs, about a nickel in U.S. currency. The student card also enabled me to ride free on German public transportation.

Berlin was an exciting city in those days. I was naively unaware

Beating Time

of the dire political upheaval going on in the country. The Nazis were beginning to acquire more and more power. In spite of Hitler, the rampant inflation, and the impending curtain of doom hanging over the city, life went on. Theaters, concert halls, cabarets, nightclubs—all were thriving.

Great teachers and performers were part of the musical life of the city—world-renowned names like the violinists Carl Flesch, Max Rostal, Karl Klingler, Adolph Busch, Simon Goldberg, and Bronislaw Huberman, and the pianists Artur Schnabel, Edwin Fischer, and Leonid Kreutzer. Bruno Walter, Otto Klemperer, Erich Kleiber, and Wilhelm Furtwängler conducted the Berlin Philharmonic and the Berlin Opera. Composers included such names as Paul Hindemith, Arnold Schönberg, and Richard Strauss. At least two operas were playing each night, and two symphony orchestras. Kurt Weill and Friedrich Holländer were producing new light operas periodically at the Cabaret der Komiker.

I was getting more proficient in German and tried to speak it all the time. I was doing fine in school. There were classes at the Hochschule, hours of practice, chamber music recitals with school friends, concerts, the opera, movies. I was young and homesick. I wrote to my mother all the time. My friends Russell and Clara Cook, on a European tour, came to Berlin especially to see me. We went to the theater, an unforgettable performance of *Das Drei Maderl Haus*, an opera based on the life of Schubert and starring the great German tenor Richard Tauber.

I made time to attend the famous piano master classes of Artur Schnabel. Three friends of mine from Boston, Charlie O'Neill, Henry Clay, and Ruth Culbertson, were studying with Schnabel, and through them I was given permission to attend. Schnabel's lessons would begin at four in the afternoon, with an intermission about seven-thirty, when Mrs. Schnabel would serve refreshments. (Mrs. Schnabel, the former Theresa Baer, was an exquisite soprano who once performed Schubert's *Winterreisse*, with Schnabel accompanying her, for all of us in their home.) The lessons would last until eleven o'clock, and during this seven-hour stretch, Schnabel would teach only three students while the others sat around, mostly on the floor, to absorb what they could. Ruth Culbertson and I prepared the Brahms D Minor Sonata and persuaded Schnabel to coach us. It was a memorable two-and-a-half-hour experience. At one point in the lesson Schnabel asked Ruth, "Where did you get that idiotic fingering?" Ruth pointed to the printed page. "Who is the idiotic editor?" he asked, then read on the cover, "Edited by Artur Schnabel." "I guess I am the idiot," he said sheepishly, "but I have changed my mind since then."

Years later, when I met Schnabel's son Karl Ulrich, he said: "You're the one! Papa used to boast about giving a lesson to a violinist!"

At the urging of Jane's mother, I had left Fraulein Winkler's and moved to a villa in the Wilmersdorf section of Berlin, where Jane and her mother had stayed. The owners of the villa, Herr and Frau Tils, were a middle-aged German couple who had no children and rented out various rooms, not for the money but because they loved people. They provided a room for me in the basement where I could practice all day without disturbance.

This was a jolly house, filled with interesting people. We all assembled around a huge table for meals where anecdotes and stories were exchanged. The main meal was in the afternoon, and at night sandwiches would be served. I was encouraged to tell American jokes in German to the delight of the others. They used to laugh uproariously, more at my bad German than at the jokes.

Beating Time

Mrs. Tils, a big, buxom woman, believed in astrology, and if she read that a certain day was bad for her, she would stay in bed all day. "The cards tell me that you are going to marry Jane," she once told me. I laughed at her. "Nonsense," I said.

After the war, when I returned to Berlin while on tour with the Boston Symphony Orchestra in 1955, I visited Frau Tils, who was still living at the villa, which had been used as a facility for the U.S. Army during the war. The house was pockmarked here and there from shelling during the war but generally unscathed. I asked her in German, "Do you recognize me?"

"Oh, little Harry, who used to practice all the time," she replied.

"Mrs. Tils," I told her, "I married Jane."

"Oh," she said, "I knew that. My cards told me."

Politics were rarely discussed at the Tilses' house. Herr Tils, the director of a match factory, had been a U-boat commander in World War I, and was still convinced that the Allies had not won the war. "Nein, nein!" he would buttonhole me. "The Americans did not win, the Germans lost!" and his bald head would glisten. Frau Tils would scold him for discussing the war, and I would remain unimpressed. I was indifferent to politics and said, "Herr Tils, it doesn't matter to me."

As far as I could tell, none of the people at the Tilses' villa were members of the Nazi party. If the name of Hitler was mentioned at all there was usually silence. Herr Tils at the time had only utter disdain for Hitler. He brought home a recording one evening of a Hitler speech, which he denounced in no uncertain terms. "Why, he doesn't even speak good German!" Tils declared. But by the time I left Germany a year later, Herr Tils had become a Nazi.

Either I was naive or ill informed, but the question of anti-

Semitism in Germany was not focused in my mind. I remember attending a party with Germans on New Year's Eve and the people were very hospitable. There was even a gift on the Christmas tree for the young American visitor. A disparaging remark had been made about Hitler, who at the time was just coming into prominence. A few minutes later there was a telephone call, and when the woman of the house returned from taking the call she was visibly upset. The caller had told her that someone at the party had insulted the Führer and that her house would be burned down. Obviously, there had been an informer at the party.

I stayed at the Tilses' villa for about six months. Then, when they announced that they were closing their home to take an extended trip, everyone moved out and I had to find new lodgings. For the next year, until my return to the United States, I lived with the Nathan family. The Nathans were a solid Jewish family whose German ancestry could be traced back many generations. Herr Nathan, who had been a decorated army officer in World War I, dismissed Hitler as a raving madman.

Life in Berlin in the Thirties

Once, when I was practicing, Alex Katz, a fellow boarder, knocked on my door. "Come on," he said, "let's go to the Femina." The Femina was a dance hall that used to stay open night and day. I couldn't imagine those things happening in the middle of the afternoon, a big dance hall and a full orchestra playing. We sat up in the balcony and on the floor every table had a telephone, a lamp, and a number. Women used to come in by themselves. You could look down on the tables and if someone appealed to you,

Beating Time

call her on the telephone and ask her to dance. I was just a kid and didn't know any better, and did a crazy thing. I called a woman on the phone and then was too shy to go down.

One night I went with a group of people to the El Dorado, which was, unbeknownst to me, a homosexual nightclub. My friends dared me to dance with one of the beautiful girls. I tried to do some fancy steps with this girl, telling her in German, "This is the latest step from America." "Ich tanze nur fornehm," she replied, "I only dance properly." It suddenly occurred to me that "she" was a man!

5

A Dream Fulfilled: Berlin to Kiev

꒱ Since my childhood days I had dreamed of someday visiting my parents' birthplace. There were no classes at the Hochschule during August, so in August 1932, having been in Berlin for more than half a year, I decided to fulfill that wish and travel to the small town of Kozeletz in the Ukraine, in what was then the Soviet Union.

Individual travel to the Soviet Union was expensive in those days and quite beyond my means. The communist authorities, however, anxious to have students visit the Soviet Union to see the "worker's paradise," offered inexpensive fares for student groups. A clerk at the official Soviet travel agency, Intourist, arranged for me to travel inexpensively with a group of Dutch students.

We left Berlin by train and traveled all night, arriving in Warsaw in the morning, where we had to transfer to a Russian train. While the change was being made I had some time to walk through the drab, dull streets of Warsaw. The sleeping car on the Russian train was infested with bugs. I had to tie up my pajamas to keep them from crawling up my legs.

After we left Warsaw on the way to Leningrad I had an opportu-

Beating Time

nity to become acquainted with the Dutch students on the tour, all of whom spoke English. I also met and spent considerable time with Scott Nearing. Now something of a cult figure, Nearing, who was about fifty at the time, was a well-known and controversial character in the early years of this century. An economist by profession, Nearing was also a socialist, pacifist, and radical who earned the great displeasure of the U.S. government by advocating resistance to the draft during World War I. Before his death in 1983 at age one hundred, Nearing authored some fifty books. He and his wife, Helen, herself a well-known author of books on independent living, both vegetarians, lived as self-sufficient organic farmers in Vermont. I immediately recognized Nearing because he had spoken at the Ford Hall Forum in Boston on a night when I had been a soloist there while a student at the New England Conservatory of Music.

When I told some of the Dutch students of Nearing's presence, they excitedly asked him to give a series of talks on the train to Leningrad. Nearing suggested that we room together when we reached Leningrad, since the officials put two to a room. Although by that time Nearing was no longer a member of the Communist party, the Soviet officials nevertheless recognized him and treated him respectfully. Soon after his arrival, his books appeared in the windows of Soviet bookstores.

Scott Nearing was an idealist. He once woke me up at midnight and made me go outside to listen to a group of street musicians. "I want you to see that they are not passing the hat," he said. Although an atheist, Nearing was one of the kindest human beings I ever knew. We sat at a big gathering one day listening to a talk by a Russian official. Glasses of tea were being served from a big samovar, but when there wasn't enough to go around, Scott re-

A Dream Fulfilled: Berlin to Kiev

fused his glass. "If not everyone has it, I don't need it," he said, gently.

Our itinerary was Leningrad, Dnepestroy, Moscow, and then Kiev. In Leningrad we were taken to view collective farms. At one stop we saw a munitions factory, and in Moscow we saw the Kremlin and Lenin's tomb. I left the tour group at Kiev, for it was from there I could reach the village of my parents' birth, Kozeletz.

I had written ahead before I left for Russia—in Yiddish—to a cousin of my mother's, Yael, who lived in Kiev. Yael was supposed to meet me at the railroad station in Kiev, but he never received my letter and wasn't there. I had his address and somehow, with the help of an Intourist official who gave me some kopeks and put me on a streetcar, I found his house. It was not much of a house, sort of a basement hovel.

Yael looked exactly like my grandfather, beard and all. He was happy to see me, especially when I showed him the gifts I had brought for him: a pair of silk pajamas (he was astonished when I told him they were for sleeping; "I will wear them on a hot day," he said), a pair of zippered galoshes for the winter; and a fountain pen, the likes of which he had never seen. (Earlier, at the border, the customs officer had wanted to know why I was carrying galoshes in the middle of summer. I told him that I had trouble with my feet and sometimes had to wear them.) The galoshes brought tears to Yael's eyes. "Please," Yael said about my gifts, "don't tell anyone. They will steal them."

Yael had two daughters, one of whom accompanied me to Kozeletz. While in Kiev I was taken by Yael to visit his other daughter, who was married to the warden of a prison farm outside the city, Rubishevskoya Kolonya. I spent the night there, a unique experience. While we were having supper, there came a knock on

Beating Time

the door. The warden went to answer it and I heard him speak angrily to the caller. I asked him about it (I had to converse in Yiddish with his wife, who translated to Russian for her husband) and was told that the prisoner had come to inquire about his furlough. Prisoners, it seemed, received two weeks' furlough every year when they could go back to their families; according to the warden, they always returned. When I inquired as to the nature of the man's crime I was told, matter-of-factly, that he had murdered his wife. "What was his sentence?" I asked. "Two years," was the reply. When I voiced my astonishment at the light sentence, the warden said, "But you did not know his wife!"

Tickets for the bus from Kiev to Kozeletz were very hard to come by; one had to make reservations for them months in advance. The warden told me to go back to my hotel and wait. The next day he sent one of the prisoners with my tickets. I attempted to engage the convict in conversation, and to my delight found he spoke Yiddish. When I asked him why he was in prison, he told me that he had been the bookkeeper for an industrial firm that, through his negligence, had gone bankrupt. "What was your sentence?" I asked. "Two years," he replied. In the Soviet Union two years seemed to be the standard sentence for crimes ranging from murdering your wife to poor bookkeeping.

Kozeletz is a small town about seventy miles from Kiev, at that time a sort of marketplace where people came each week to sell their produce and other goods. A number of people in Kozeletz, some related, remembered my parents and grandparents. I was shown the houses where both my father and mother were born. I also visited the synagogue they had attended. The wife of the shamus (sexton) even remembered them. "You look just like your fa-

A Dream Fulfilled: Berlin to Kiev

ther," she said and pointed out where both my grandparents sat in the *schul.*

As I left the synagogue I was surrounded by the entire town of Kozeletz, all claiming to be relatives! One, a man with an enormous head, I recognized from my parents' description as "Moshe with the two heads." Moshe was the town's intellectual, and he immediately engaged me in conversation about American history. "Ah," he said, "Boston! Bonker Hill?" and I had to admit that I had never been to Bunker Hill.

The evening of my departure from Kozeletz, Yael's daughter and I waited in the village square for the bus from Chernigov to take us back to Kiev, where I was to join the tour group for the return trip to Berlin. The bus finally arrived; the driver stopped, opened the door, announced the bus was full, and drove off!

Told that the next bus would not come until the following evening, I was in a quandary; I had to be back in Kiev in the morning to rejoin the tour. Then a fellow named Mottel Manyilov offered to drive us in his horse and wagon to Oster, a town on the Dnieper River whence we could take the night boat to Kiev.

Oster was about eighteen miles away, and it was almost midnight when we got there. Mottel told me that this was the same wagon that took my parents some twenty years earlier on their way to America. And from the looks of the animal, it was the same horse, too!

When we got to the dock I paid Mottel, thanked him profusely, and sent him back to Kozeletz. We found ourselves, Yael's daughter and I, on board a ferry being loaded with Red Army soldiers and their supplies. We found seats on a sack of potatoes and sat there until we reached Kiev at six o'clock in the morning.

Beating Time

With the help of Yael's daughter, I got back to my hotel in time for our group's departure, only to be informed that my passport was not in order and that I would have to stay behind. It seemed the Intourist office in Berlin had neglected to add the name of the exiting town, Shepetovka, to my passport. For two days I hung around Kiev, not being told when I would be allowed to leave. In the meantime I was taken to a photographer for new passport photos, then summoned before a commissar to answer questions I did not understand. Since I spoke no Russian and the commissar no English, we conversed in German. "Why is your passport different from all the others?" "Where were you born?" "Where was your father born?" To say I was uneasy is putting it mildly. Finally I was given permission to leave.

I returned to Berlin in September 1932 and resumed my practicing and study at the Hochschule. On February 5, 1933, I went with the Nathan family to Potsdam to witness the formal inauguration of Adolf Hitler as chancellor of Germany. One week earlier he had been appointed to the post by the second president of the Weimar Republic, General Paul von Hindenburg.

Hindenburg, who was eighty-six years old at the time, seemed to be a doddering old man as he sat on the platform nodding off. Herr Nathan, a man in his early fifties, a decorated World War I hero, sat ramrod stiff, his numerous decorations proudly displayed on his chest. As a German he was proud, as a Jew apprehensive. The growing anti-Semitism of the Nazis could not be directed to him, he thought. "It must be the Eastern Jews, the Poles and the Russians." He was reassured at the ceremony by the appearance onstage of, among the other dignitaries, Hermann Tiez, the owner of Berlin's largest department store, the Kaufhaus des Westens—popularly known as the Ka-De-We—and one of the city's wealthi-

A Dream Fulfilled: Berlin to Kiev

est Jews. Herr Nathan told me, pointing to his medals, that he would come to no harm. He could not have foreseen his death a few years later in a Nazi concentration camp.

On February 27 the seat of the German government, the Reichstag, was burned down, and even German Jews were horrified. Herr Nathan wailed, "What is happening to our beloved Reichstag?" I could see the flames from where I was living. I remember the next day little fliers appeared on the benches in the park at Bayerischenplatz. "Who set fire to the Reichstag?" the fliers asked. "Hermann Göring and his S.S. men." These fliers were swiftly gathered up and destroyed by uniformed Nazis.

On April 1, 1933, the day of the infamous boycott, I saw young Nazis in their brown uniforms with pails of red paint smear the windows of supposedly Jewish shops with Stars of David and the word *Jude*. One owner of a butcher shop whose windows had been painted came out screaming, "But I'm not Jewish!" The Nazis screamed back, "You look Jewish!" I witnessed one act of courage outside the shop of Loesser and Wolff, Tobacconists. A man came out and upon seeing the Nazis with the boycott signs, showed them his backside. "That's what you people deserve," he said. He was immediately hauled away.

Conditions in Berlin were deteriorating, and many, especially Jews, were beginning to make plans to leave. Some members of the Nathan family had already left for Holland, where, as it later turned out, they were no safer than in Germany. The remaining members of the Nathan family were eventually taken to a concentration camp, where they died. The Nazis were present everywhere, but rightly or not, I had no fear of physical harm because I wore an American flag on my lapel.

I read one day in the newspaper that Joseph Goebbels, the Nazi

Beating Time

minister of propaganda, had forbidden Bruno Walter to conduct the Berlin Philharmonic the following Sunday. Until then I had no idea that Walter was Jewish. In Walter's stead the aged Richard Strauss was engaged. Even though I felt I should not attend the concert, the opportunity of seeing the legendary Strauss compelled me to go. The hall, usually full, was three-quarters empty. The frail Strauss conducted sitting on a high stool, and very perfunctorily. He looked as if he were going to fall asleep. The old Strauss adage, "conductors should never perspire; only the musicians should sweat," came to mind.

I had heard that some of my own countrymen were sympathizing with Hitler, but I was shocked one evening to hear a radio speech in German by the American actor Adolphe Menjou at a dinner in his honor given by Goebbels. Even our own hero Charles Lindbergh came to Berlin as a guest of Hermann Göring to praise the Nazis.

Slowly at first, then with growing rapidity, the composers and musicians, conductors and pedagogues who had made Berlin the musical capital of the world began to flee. In the spring of 1933 I had had enough of Germany and decided to go back to the United States. My parents had been writing constantly urging me to return. Jane had already left and was back in New Rochelle.

Before leaving Berlin I called the Tilses, who invited me to dinner. Herr Tils seemed to be very apologetic. "Please don't talk harshly about us in the United States. This too will pass."

The persecution of the Jews in Germany seemed to be an anomaly. For generations German Jews had considered themselves superior to Jews from other countries. When the full force of anti-Semitism became apparent, even the German Jews themselves underestimated its extent. "It is against the Eastern Jews," they thought. "We are Germans." Jewish assimilation in Germany was higher than anywhere in the world, and in many families all traces of Jewish ethnicity had been erased. Yet in their diabolical thoroughness, the Nazis were able to trace back through many generations even a hint of a Jewish connection.

I came home in May 1933, on a sister ship of the *Scythia*, the Cunard liner *Laconia*, depressed and uncertain of my future.

6

Return to Reality

❦ Returning home from Germany was an emotional and bewildering experience. As the ship moved into the dock at Boston, I spotted my parents from the upper deck and waved frantically. I was standing behind a low railing and my mother could not see my lower body. "Look," she said to my father. "He's lost his legs!" My mother fainted; there were no half measures of emotion in our family. I came down the gangplank into my mother's arms (by then revived) and we embraced. There were no words spoken, but copious tears were shed.

It was good to be home, but now what? I was twenty-four years old, had an extensive musical education and background, but no job. Although my heart was set on the Boston Symphony Orchestra, I had no idea if any vacancies existed and no prospects of an audition with the unapproachable conductor of the orchestra, Serge Koussevitzky.

My dear friend Russell Ames Cook came to the rescue. He introduced me to Joseph Lee, a legendary figure in Boston's political scene who had dedicated his life to public service, especially to the youth of the city. At the time Mr. Lee was the director of Community Recreation Service, an organization concerned with

Beating Time

recreational activities in greater Boston. The organization had just
received a grant from the Federal Music Project, a program of the
Works Progress Administration.

The Works Progress Administration, or WPA, was one of the
federal government programs created by President Franklin Del-
ano Roosevelt to provide relief to the millions of Americans unemployed as a result of the Great Depression. The WPA is mostly
remembered for its construction projects, and today, some sixty
years later, the tangible results of that effort are still evident in the
hundreds of bridges, roads, and public buildings still in use. But
the director of the WPA, Harry Hopkins, also wanted to employ
the skills of artists and writers. This desire resulted in the creation
of three special programs—the Federal Writers', Theater, and
Art Projects.

The Federal Music Project, incorporated as part of the art project, was headed by Dr. Nicolai Sokoloff, the conductor of the
Cleveland Orchestra, and had on its advisory board Walter Dam-
rosch, George Gershwin, Leopold Stokowski, and Lawrence Tib-
bett, among others. The Boston member of the board was Wallace
Goodrich of the New England Conservatory. Arthur Fiedler, the
conductor of the Boston Pops, was also active in the project as a
guest conductor, and it was here that I first met Arthur, with whom
I was later to have a very close association.

What the Federal Art Project did for the arts in America was
truly remarkable. For the first time in our nation's history, years
before the creation of the National Endowment for the Arts, the
federal government was directly supporting artists. Before it was
disbanded in 1943, the music project employed fifteen thousand
musicians in symphony orchestras, bands, chamber music ensem-

Return to Reality

bles, dance companies, operas, and choruses, as well as copyists, arrangers, librarians, and one composers' group.

In Boston there were three WPA symphony orchestras: the Commonwealth Symphony, the State Symphony, and the Women's Symphony (women were not yet integrated into the all-male symphony orchestras). All three performed free concerts, indoors and outdoors, throughout greater Boston. There was also an opera company, under the direction of Ernst Hoffman, giving performances of all the standard repertoire at the Boston Opera House. The Commonwealth Chorus, under the direction of A. Buckingham Simpson, gave numerous concerts in churches and auditoriums throughout the city.

My involvement with the WPA was through my association with the Community Recreation Service, for which I had been supervising amateur orchestras and choruses throughout the city. Adding to this job, after receiving the grant from the Federal Music Project, I set about the business of establishing an orchestra of unemployed professional musicians. In a short time an orchestra of questionable balance was formed, and rehearsals, which I conducted, began to take place at the community center on Blossom Street in the West End. There were two criteria for admittance to the orchestra: ability and need, the former by audition, the latter by proof.

"Proof of need" soon became a stumbling block. Although we engaged numbers of good out-of-work musicians, some young, some old, certain sections of the orchestra had to be filled with players who did not quite "need" the job; rather, we needed them. I remember calling Washington and speaking to an official who didn't know what an oboe was. When I asked for permission to

Beating Time

hire one, he said, "What do you need an oboe for? They're a dime a dozen." I finally had to appeal to Nicolai Sokoloff, and we were given permission to engage "un-needy" players.

For the next four years I was part of a thriving musical scene in Boston. Many of those young musicians later took their places in major orchestras and opera companies, men and women of the caliber of Jerome Lipson, viola; George Zazofsky, violin; and James Pappoutsakis, flute, all of whom eventually joined the Boston Symphony Orchestra. One of the young singers, Eleanor Steber, later became a leading star with the Metropolitan Opera.

While I was busy in Boston, Jane Goldberg was working as a counselor at the Hebrew Sheltering and Guardian Society in Pleasantville, New York, a home for orphaned Jewish children. We wrote to each other frequently—long-distance telephoning was too exotic and expensive in those days. There were frequent drives to and from Pleasantville. Jane drove into Boston one day in a two-seater Model T Ford. Where she got the car, I don't know, but she had just received her driver's license and was scared to death. She took the train back to New York, leaving the car for me to drive back.

I was still a reluctant suitor, because my teachers' admonition not to get "involved" remained strong in my mind. But I also knew that Jane had to become part of my life. "Are we engaged now?" she would ask, and I would avoid answering her. My mother noticed my demeanor during those days and took an unusual role for a Jewish mother, urging her son to marry someone she had never met. Finally, one day in Franklin Park in Boston, I gave Jane a ring. Again she asked, "Are we engaged now?" and still I avoided the answer.

After a year of back-and-forth travel, Jane and I decided to get

Return to Reality

married. My mother and father; my younger sister, Lil; and my uncle Percy and aunt Ida drove from Boston for the wedding. Jane's mother and father attended, as did Jane's uncle and aunt, Sol and Hilda Stroock, and my dear friends Russell and Clara Cook. My older sister, Ruth, was too pregnant at the time to attend.

We were married on October 13, 1935, in the Free Synagogue in New York City, in the study of Rabbi Stephen Wise. Rabbi Wise was an eminent public figure, a great orator, a confidant of President Roosevelt, and a man of considerable influence. He was a friend of Jane's mother and father and had been instrumental in Jane's adoption.

The day before the ceremony, Jane and I had visited with Rabbi Wise and asked him to make the wedding ceremony as short as possible. "I can do it in about three minutes," he assured me. My Orthodox mother had never seen such a short Jewish wedding and was rather taken aback when it was over. There was no traditional chupa (canopy), no yarmulkes, no chanting. She had taught me the Hebrew wedding vow, which I recited, much to the astonishment of the rabbi, who said afterward that it was the first time he had ever encountered a groom who knew the words in Hebrew and from memory. In deference to my parents, a wine glass wrapped in a napkin had been supplied, which I crushed at the end of the ceremony. My mother took it all reservedly. "Are you really married?" she asked. "He's a rabbi; I suppose he knows what he's doing."

After the wedding there was a dinner at the then-famous French restaurant Charles in Greenwich Village. Jane and I then drove to Ossining, New York, the summer home of Hilda and Sol Stroock. We stayed at a small cottage on the estate, and Aunt Hilda had thoughtfully provided a maid to serve our meals. We spent a week there, occasionally driving to New York at night. On one of these nights we were the guests of my cousin, Eddie Duchin, at his weekly Texaco radio show on NBC. We returned to Boston and got a small apartment on Lothian Road in the Brighton section of Boston, and I resumed my WPA job.

I did a combination of conducting and administration and also played solos under other conductors. I remember five performances in one week of the Mendelssohn Violin Concerto and the Chausson *Poème*. I also played and conducted many concerts at the Gardner Museum, some as soloist with piano accompaniment, some with various chamber groups—the Stradivarius Quartet, the Malkin Trio, the Zimbler Sinfonietta. In 1937 I conducted the Boston premiere of Shostakovich's First Piano Concerto at the Gardner Museum with the Commonwealth Symphony Orchestra. The pianist was Frederic Tillotson, and the solo trumpeter was Vic Ferri.

During my long association with the Gardner Museum I enjoyed a friendship with Morris Carter, the director of the museum. Mr. Carter, a typical reserved New England Yankee and proper Bostonian, had been Mrs. Gardner's secretary while she assembled the art collection and built the museum. I had a few difficulties with him because of his utter dislike for "modern" music, which for him meant anything composed after Debussy. I once played a new piece by a young Hungarian composer. "Don't ever play that piece here again!" he admonished. A year later I sneaked it into another program and Carter said, "That was an interesting piece, Harry. You should play it again."

I must have been a very busy young man in those days. I even found time to teach one day a week at the Brookline Music School. Two of my pupils went on to play in the New York Phil-

Return to Reality

harmonic Orchestra, while one, Mike Wallace, became famous in
another field. There were also occasional appearances at the Sunday evening meetings of the Ford Hall Forum. I played anywhere
and everywhere.

For most of my life it had been my burning ambition to play in
the Boston Symphony Orchestra. Symphony Hall was for me a
shrine. I used to tip my hat when I passed it. How to get in? Or
at least get an audition with the orchestra's conductor, Serge
Koussevitzky? In those days there were no formal auditions or no-
tices of auditions. Whenever there was a vacancy in the orchestra,
an applicant had to gain access to Koussevitzky somehow in order
to audition for him. My audition was arranged for me by a wonderful lady, Sylvia Dreyfus, a talented sculptor and charming
champion of the arts, who was also a close friend of Koussevitzky's. She simply asked him to hear me play, and an audition was
granted for a certain Saturday morning—a cold wintry day early
in 1938.

7

A Half Century with the Boston Symphony Orchestra

༄ I arrived at Symphony Hall at the appointed time and was ushered into Koussevitzky's green room, a room set aside for the orchestra's conductor, where all the first players of the orchestra sat around, looking like pallbearers. Accompanied by Arthur Fiedler, I played the first movement of a Mozart concerto, then the Glazunov Concerto. About halfway through the Glazunov I was stopped and the inevitable sight-reading began.

On the table were a number of first violin parts, one of which Koussey placed on the stand. It was a Mozart symphony, rather easy. Then came a more difficult piece and a Richard Strauss tone poem, which I fortunately had practiced ahead of time. Koussey kept saying, "Good," and I began to relax, until he called Leslie Rogers, the orchestra's librarian, and said, "Rogers, please bring me the Taneyev symphony."

Not only had I never played the piece, but I had never even heard of Taneyev. As a matter of fact, I don't think Koussey knew the piece very well either. I plowed through that very difficult composition. In those days I was a pretty good sight reader, and

Beating Time

to this day I am not sure if Koussey knew whether I was playing the right notes. But again he said, "Good," and the audition was over. Koussevitzky asked me to wait outside, and in a few minutes he came out of the green room and asked me to come back in April, the last morning of the orchestra's season. When I asked him if he wanted to hear me again, he replied that it would not be necessary.

On the last day of the season, a Saturday morning, I arrived at Symphony Hall and stood in the corridor outside the green room. Leslie Rogers, a purveyor of doom and gloom, asked if I had brought my violin. I said no, to which Rogers replied, "Well, there are around twenty violinists in there playing for him." My heart sank as I stood there, listening through the closed door to some impressive fiddling. Finally Koussey came out, saw me, and said, "Dickson, I look for you. You are still the best. You know we have no vacancy, but I make a place for you." With that he took me to the office of George Judd, the orchestra's manager, and said, "Mr. Judd, this is our new member of the orchestra." Thus began my forty-nine years as a player with the Boston Symphony Orchestra, and as a player and conductor with the Boston Pops, an association that has continued for well over a half century.

The contract arrived a few days later. It was for forty weeks of employment—thirty with the Symphony and ten with the Pops—at a salary of seventy dollars per week. In those days before withholding tax and social security deductions, I got the full amount. Each check was exactly the same, with my name and the amount printed on it. The only other checks ever issued were the occasional recording checks. At that time, in 1938, the BSO was recording exclusively for RCA Victor. The fee for each musician, except the first-chair players, was fifteen dollars for a three-hour

A Half Century with the Boston Symphony Orchestra

session. Today things are much different. The basic annual salary for a member of the BSO is well over fifty thousand dollars, plus generous recording fees and fees for radio and television appear-- ances. All of this is in addition to the player's outside musical activities.

The culmination of my dream to become a violinist with the Boston Symphony Orchestra began with a rehearsal in Symphony Hall under Koussevitzky of Beethoven's Ninth Symphony in preparation for the opening concert at Tanglewood. This would be the third year of the Boston Symphony Orchestra's summer concerts at Tanglewood, in the Berkshire Mountains of western Massachusetts. For a number of years before that, a group of affluent New Yorkers who summered in the Berkshires had engaged Henry Hadley to conduct members of the New York Philharmonic in a series of outdoor concerts called the Berkshire Music Festival. The sponsors of the festival wanted to expand it and invited Arthur Fiedler to come down and look things over. Koussevitzky heard about it and expressed an interest in establishing a summer music festival sponsored by the BSO. In 1936 the Berkshire Music Festival severed its ties with the New York Philharmonic and engaged Koussevitzky and the BSO to give an expanded program of twelve concerts each season. Initially the orchestra played under a tent on an estate in the Berkshires at Lenox, Massachusetts. In 1937 disaster struck. During one of the concerts it rained so hard that the tent leaked and a violent thunderstorm competed with the sound of the orchestra. Koussey made an impassioned speech in his distinctively accented English, threatening not to come back unless suitable accommodations were provided.

The chairman of the festival, and a regular at the performances, Gertrude Robinson-Smith, promised Koussey an auditorium and

Beating Time

set about raising the necessary funds. By the summer of 1938 a fine five-thousand-seat auditorium, an early creation of the famous Finnish-born American architect and designer Eero Saarinen, was completed at Tanglewood. My first concert, the first of more than a thousand to follow, was in the new Tanglewood Shed.

On the day of my first rehearsal with the BSO, after being introduced by Koussey from my place in the back of the second violins, I was filled with pride and had a fierce headache. Today the headache is gone, but the pride remains.

During my almost half century as a player with the BSO, the eleven years under Serge Koussevitzky still stand out. His enormous influence on the orchestra continues to be felt to this day.

Koussevitzky first came to Boston in 1925 and stayed for fifty years, longer than any other conductor in the orchestra's history. Koussevitzky's background was rather mysterious. It was known that he had conducted orchestras in Russia, then later in France. In his teens he attended the Moscow Conservatory as a bass player, played in the orchestra, and later became known as a great virtuoso on that unwieldy instrument.

Very little else was known about his early years. Koussey played the part of the grand seigneur, the untouchable aristocrat, and undoubtedly believed in his own divinity. Born of humble Jewish background, Koussey changed his religion as a matter of necessity to Russian Orthodox when, as a student at the Moscow Conservatory, he was forced to do so in order to be able to live in the Russian capital.

Shortly after his arrival in Boston, Koussevitzky was interviewed by the press. One of the reporters from a local Jewish newspaper, the *Jewish Daily Forward,* asked him if he were Jewish. Koussey's reply was noncommittal. "Is that important in this country?" he asked. "Why do not the others ask about my religion?" This reply did not endear him to the Jewish community. As far as anyone knows, Koussevitzky did not practice any formal religion. During his final year with the BSO, however, he called his friend Carl Dreyfus on Yom Kippur and asked to be taken to an Orthodox Jewish synagogue. Carl drove him to an old *shul* in the West End of Boston. No one recognized Koussevitzky. He sat in a back row for an hour, deep in thought, then quietly whispered to Carl to take him home.

Koussevitzky's life was like a play in which he acted his part with conviction. He whole life seemed to have been a circle. Born a Jew, his funeral service was conducted in an Episcopal Church by a Russian Orthodox priest. He was buried in a Congregational churchyard in the Berkshires, and the headstone on his grave was a gift from the state of Israel.

What kind of a conductor was Serge Alexandrovich Koussevitzky? He was a dedicated egomaniac who believed himself immortal. He had unquestioning faith in himself and in his orchestra. In my mind he was the greatest leader I have ever known, able through the power of his own conviction to inspire a person to play better than he knew he could. (At that time there were no "shes" in the orchestra.) He instilled in every member of the orchestra the feeling that we were all consummate artists and that the BSO was the only orchestra in the world. Yet there was a streak of sadism in Koussevitzky. Occasionally he would ask each member of the violin section to play a particularly difficult passage alone (a practice later forbidden by union rules). He seemed to be somewhat deflated if they acquitted themselves well. "Good!" he would acknowledge reluctantly. Although Koussey never fired anyone, there was always that fear.

Beating Time

Koussevitzky's directives were given in an indescribable jargon. "Gentlemen, you play di notes in time, but vot iss betveen di times you not care!" "Ve vill rehearse tousand times over and over until ve not have dat vot is need!" "Clarinet, vy do you propose to me a sonority dat do not belong to us?" And on and on it went, nobody seemingly aware of the massacre of the English language. As a matter of fact, I discovered in the tuning room during intermission the same picturesque language among my new colleagues. "Kolya, you got twice mutes?" "No, I got only vonce."

I soon got used to the cacophony in the tuning room. During intermission, while some were blowing or fiddling, others were quietly studying their instruments with frustration. In one corner of the room, a clarinetist sat trying out reeds. An oboist sat in another corner with his scalpel fashioning a reed, which he inserted and blew, then, making a face, started shaving again. A violinist, a backstage soloist, was busily fiddling in a corner; I found out he gave a whole recital for himself during the intermission. Some had strange ways of practicing. Daniel Eisler, a fine Russian violinist, stood in front of his locker and played interminable high notes over and over again, and the resulting squeaks caused Benny Fiedler, the orchestra cynic, to remark, "Eisler is telegraphing to China again."

In those days most of the musicians in the BSO were Europeans. There was a dignity about all the players in the orchestra. They used to come to the concerts in their black homburg hats and fur-collared coats. They dressed at home. Nowadays the kids in the orchestra wouldn't be caught dead in a homburg, or on the street in their symphony clothes, which they leave in lockers in Symphony Hall. They come to play in sneakers and jeans.

Strangely enough, with all the glamour that was attached to

A Half Century with the Boston Symphony Orchestra

those great European virtuosi, our modern players are actually superior. The technique of musical performance has developed tremendously in the past hundred years. What used to be considered a professional level of playing would not pass today. In the early days American virtuosi were European trained. Today's young American players study in the States, and with American teachers. Moreover, foreign students are flocking to the United States. Professional musicians today are better performers, and are certainly more technically proficient, than the older generations. There are those, however, who complain that the "young Turks" lack artistic integrity and soul in their music making, a criticism with which I do not agree.

8

Temple of Music

ᶜ Koussevitzky always referred to Symphony Hall as "our temple," and indeed this wonderful hall has been, since 1900, the mecca of musical activity in Boston. Occasionally it has been the site of nonmusical affairs, such as commencement exercises, political rallies, banquets, and even private parties. Still, it remains a respected house for things artistic. Symphony Hall's perfect acoustics is no accident. It was the first concert hall ever built in conformity with modern principles of acoustics. To Professor Wallace C. Sabine, then an assistant professor of physics at Harvard, goes the credit for this achievement: an acoustical perfection furthered by the integrity of the architects McKim, Mead, and White in following Sabine's specifications. The architects respected the relationship of sound to structure and thus avoided an acoustical disaster such as would occur in the building of Avery Fisher Hall at Lincoln Center.

Symphony Hall seats 2,631 people for regular concerts, and 2,345 when the floor seats are removed and tables set up for the Pops concerts. Except for the gold organ pipes and trimming around the stage and on the balcony gratings, there is a minimum of decoration—unless, of course, one happens to glance up at the

65

Beating Time

statues surrounding the auditorium high above the second balcony. Although the niches were important aspects of the entire acoustical scheme, the addition of undraped statues was a happy afterthought. For those of prudish sensibilities let me add that they were selected by a committee of two hundred of the most proper Bostonians, headed by the most proper of all, Mrs. J. W. Elliot.

When Symphony Hall opened for its first concert in September 1900, the statues were not yet in place, but were added gradually as they came from the studio of Pietro Caproni of Boston. They are copies of famous statues of ancient Rome and Greece and add much to the dignity of the hall, the disparaging remarks of far-sighted New Yorkers notwithstanding. To us in the orchestra, they have become old friends who give no greeting and expect none. We know they are there, guarding our cultural heritage, and we hardly ever look up at them. I daresay there are some of my colleagues who have never even noticed them. After forty-three years in the orchestra, Benny Fiedler did notice them once during a Pops concert. "Look, Bixsen," said Benny, who had a nickname for everyone, during the final measure of Handel's Largo, as he suddenly looked up at the Amazon of Polycletus. "She's scratching herself!" Then, as we came to the final G-major chord, "And the other one has no pants!"

There are five chandeliers at Symphony Hall, one in each corner and one in the center. The corner ones have four tiers of spokes; the middle one has five. Each of the spokes holds an electric light bulb at its end. During moments of less than full concentration at concerts (especially in choral works when the orchestra has nothing to play) I have wickedly attempted to count the bulbs,

Temple of Music

but never quite made it. Our electrician at Symphony Hall has supplied me with the following facts:

Each of the corner chandeliers contains 71 spokes and bulbs, while the center one has 111, making a total of 395. The bulbs are changed twice a year: before the symphony season and before the Pops in the spring. For a long time I wondered, as have other distracted music lovers, how in the world this is done. Did someone have to climb up on a ladder? It would be a dizzying climb. My curiosity was appeased when I came into the hall one day before the opening of the season in September and saw all the chandeliers resting on the floor, lowered by cables.

Every few years the entire hall is repainted. This is no ordinary undertaking. In order to get to the ceiling, a scaffold has to be erected, which takes the better part of a week and costs thousands of dollars. The paint colors are the same used in the original construction back in 1900. With Bostonian foresight, the planners of Symphony Hall had preserved the original formula and color samples. Even so, one supersensitive music critic detected a change in the acoustical qualities after the hall was repainted.

Each spring the lower maroon walls of the hall used to be painted green for the Pops season, then repainted in the fall for the winter concerts, a practice discontinued some years ago. This was miraculously accomplished overnight by our building crew. Since the hall was built in 1900 and each year two coats of paint were added, a little figuring will produce the startling statistic that the walls of Symphony Hall carried over a hundred and thirty coats of paint. No wonder some of our older subscribers voiced the opinion that the hall seemed to be getting narrower.

9

The BSO Goes Union

⌐ In 1938 the Boston Symphony Orchestra was the only American professional orchestra not unionized. There had been a near-disastrous strike in 1921, while Pierre Monteux was conductor. Half the orchestra had refused to go onstage for a Saturday evening performance, and the program had to be changed. The musicians lost. Those who had refused to perform were fired, then later given the chance to return. Most did return, but a number left the orchestra permanently, including the concertmaster, Frederick Fradkin, the leader of the revolt.

It goes without saying that the conservative Yankee trustees of the orchestra were vehemently opposed to any kind of unionism and did everything they could to keep the orchestra "independent." But they underestimated the power of the head of the International Musician's Union, James Caesar Petrillo. Petrillo's reputation was that of an irascible gangster. His frustration was that the great Boston Symphony Orchestra, for which he had the utmost respect, was not in the union. He embarked on a campaign to force the issue.

In the early 1940s Petrillo succeeded in organizing the soloists, who were then forbidden to play with nonunion orchestras. For a

Beating Time

year or two the BSO gave concerts under Koussevitzky without international soloists. There was one exception, the Polish pianist Jan Smeterlin, who refused to join the union. Petrillo's next move was to "blackmail" the recording companies. If they insisted on recording the BSO, they could not record any union orchestra. As a result, for a period of time the prestigious and lucrative making of records was lost to the BSO.

The trustees and management, in desperation, decided to make their own recordings. Machinery and presses were brought into the basement of Symphony Hall. However, belated considerations of marketing, distribution, and so on convinced those in authority that the whole attempt was impractical, and the paraphernalia was removed.

By this time Koussevitzky was beginning to cave in to reality. He was bothered not only by the soloists and recording boycotts but also by his not being allowed to conduct other orchestras. One day in 1941 I received a phone call from Carl Dreyfus, Sylvia Dreyfus's husband, who was at the time the publisher of the *Boston American* newspaper. Dreyfus asked if I knew how to reach James Caesar Petrillo. I was more than surprised to hear that Koussevitzky had asked to meet with Petrillo. I gave Dreyfus Petrillo's telephone number, and within a week a meeting was arranged.

Carl Dreyfus later told me about that clandestine meeting, which took place at Koussevitzky's summer home in the Berkshires. Petrillo drove up in an armored car with three bodyguards. In addition to Koussevitzky, three trustees and Carl Dreyfus were at the meeting. Contrary to their expectations, Petrillo turned out to be charming, affable, and extremely knowledgeable about the Boston Symphony. He quoted facts and figures about the orchestra going back fifty years. There were long discussions, mainly

The BSO Goes Union

about management's concern with union interference. Petrillo promised there would be none in either artistic or policy matters. Whereas in other cities the union was the negotiating agent for the orchestra, the Boston Symphony players would be their own autonomous negotiators. (They still are today.) Petrillo seemed so anxious to add another feather to his cap that he agreed to all the stipulations of Koussevitzky and the trustees.

Meanwhile, the musicians held ongoing meetings. The majority favored the union, but a few diehards fought vigorously against it. Not until word came down that the trustees were not opposed did the musicians vote almost unanimously to become members of the American Federation of Musicians (as the union was by this time called). When that news got out, we received a telegram of congratulations from Frederick Fradkin: "At long last. Congratulations!" My father, a lifelong union man, was very happy. "Maybe now you can talk back to that czar Koussevitzky," he exclaimed.

The Koussevitzky years of the Boston Symphony Orchestra were perhaps the golden years of the orchestra. The BSO, named later by RCA Victor "The Aristocrat of Orchestras," was enjoying rapturous reviews. The two other major American orchestras, the New York Philharmonic under Arturo Toscanini and the Philadelphia Orchestra with Leopold Stokowski, were, according to Koussevitzky, no match for his innovative programming. I remember the first rehearsal of our twentieth season under Koussey, in 1945. It was a festive occasion and Koussey made the most of it. The right balcony overlooking the stage was filled with critics and reporters, and before rehearsal began Koussey delivered a speech he had prepared beforehand, extolling himself and the orchestra.

"An orchestra," he began, "is like a person. Sometimes it is very down and sometimes it is very up. Sometimes down for many

Beating Time

years and then very up. I, myself, have a high fever for ten years. Then it go away." (Here we realized he meant "hay fever.") "Let us see how very up we are in these twenty years," he continued, then listed the many new works he had introduced: works by Stravinsky, Hindemith, Schoenberg, Bartók, Copland, Harris, Piston, William Schuman, Barber, and others. "Now," he proclaimed, "let us see vot the other orchestras do," and without naming any names, he launched into a tirade against Toscanini and Stokowski.

"One conductor, he play Suppé overtures." (Toscanini had revived a number of von Suppé's light opera overtures, which some critics considered second-rate.) "And the other conductor go to the movies!" (Stokowski had appeared in a motion picture featuring himself, the Philadelphia Orchestra, and Deanna Durbin, called *One Hundred Men and a Girl.*)

Playing in a great orchestra such as the Boston Symphony is time-consuming, strenuous, and nerve-racking. There are over two hundred concerts a year, with a greater number of rehearsals. There are tours, national and international. Each concert is, of course, a serious affair, but occasionally unforeseen things happen.

We were playing Shostakovich's Fifth Symphony in Cleveland one night when a near catastrophe occurred. The piano, which in Boston was always on Koussevitzky's left, was somehow placed to his right. When, in the first movement, the pianist, Lukas Foss, began his rhythmic pattern coming from the wrong side, it threw Koussey completely off. He became so confused that he stopped conducting. After a few bars, he began to wave his arms, but no one knew exactly where we were in the score. Our second trumpet player, Marcel LaFosse, maintained afterward that he played a short solo at least three times, each time to be waved off by Koussey. The strings had nothing to play, but our concertmaster, Rich-

The BSO Goes Union

ard Burgin, decided to take the bull by the horns and led the violins into our next entrance, after a dozen measures had been skipped. Somehow the orchestra got back on track, even though an entire section was not played. The next morning we read the critics' reports of a stupendous performance of the Shostakovich Fifth Symphony.

During a performance of Brahms' Second Piano Concerto in Symphony Hall by Rudolf Serkin, there was a sudden snap as the piano's pedal broke. Serkin shrugged his shoulders and walked off-stage, to be followed back by "Zeke" Walker, the Steinway piano tuner. Zeke was blind and was led onto the stage by Harvey Genereux, our stage manager, carrying a hammer and chisel. The audience applauded. With Zeke's directives, Harvey banged away under the piano, and in eighteen minutes the piano was fixed, whereupon Zeke and Harvey left the stage to tumultuous applause. Serkin returned, and the concert resumed.

For violinists, the most common mishap during performance is a breaking string. When this happens during a violin concerto, the soloist grabs the concertmaster's violin and plays on. When the young violinist Midori was playing Bernstein's Serenade at Tanglewood, her E string snapped. Although a very young talent (only fourteen years old), she had the presence of mind to accept the concertmaster's violin and continue, only to have the E string break again. This time she took the assistant concertmaster's instrument and finished the piece. Once, Ruggiero Ricci's bow suddenly snapped at the tip while he was playing the Sibelius Concerto. He finished with the concertmaster's bow.

I look back now to the year 1938, when I entered the orchestra. How long ago that was! I even feel that I have a connection with the very first Boston Symphony of 1881. During the orchestra's

Beating Time

sixtieth anniversary in 1941, I met a player in that original orchestra. Daniel Kountz was a violinist who had played under three of the orchestra's first conductors—Georg Henschel, Wilhelm Gericke, and Arthur Nikisch. I wondered what kind of music was played in those days.

"Oh," Kountz said, "we played the usual—Mozart and Haydn and Beethoven, Schubert and Gluck."

"Did you play any modern music?" I asked.

"Oh, yes," he replied. "Especially later, under Gericke, there was a modern piece on almost every program."

"Like what?" I asked.

"Well, Dvořák, Tchaikovsky, Brahms."

Kountz related to me the experience of playing Brahms' Fourth Symphony for the first time. Nobody liked it, and Gericke had to convince the players that Brahms was a serious composer. After the first performance of the work on Friday afternoon, however, Gericke made a statement to the press saying he had removed it from the Saturday program "for further study." "It was," he told them, "completely foreign to the musicians, and they needed more time." Gericke substituted a Schumann symphony for the Saturday concert. For a long time thereafter, Brahms was not totally accepted. In fact, the eminent music critic Philip Hale wrote: "The EXIT signs in the hall should read 'In Case of Brahms.'"

10

The Life of a Musician

I felt a certain pride in being in the Boston Symphony Orchestra, as did my children when they grew older. I knew that Jane was also very proud of me, although she was never one to shower others with praise. When the children brought home good report cards from school, it was I who made a fuss over them while Jane was more restrained.

In the summer of 1957 I received a rather formal-looking communication from the French government. "Look what I just got," I said to Jane, who spoke French fluently, and asked her to read it. It was from the minister of culture informing me that I had been nominated Chevalier dans l'Ordre des Arts et des Lettres. Jane began to read it, then suddenly stopped: "Did you take out the garbage?" she asked. That was Jane!

During my first year in the orchestra, I established a routine that was to dominate my personal and professional life for fifty years. That life, and the lives of my family, revolved around the Boston Symphony. Rehearsals, concerts, and orchestra tours dictated our life-style. The children grew used to my practicing and to the frequent string quartet rehearsals in the living room when they came home from school.

Beating Time

Our social lives were intertwined with members of the orchestra and their functions. Various wives' groups met periodically, and of course the main topic of discussion was the orchestra. I would find out many interesting things about the orchestra after one of those wives' meetings.

Musicians Are Human

During my first year in the Boston Symphony I sat next to Arthur Fiedler's uncle Bernard. "Benny" had been playing in the orchestra for over forty years and had become jaded and cynical. He was not, to say the least, as thrilled at being in the Boston Symphony Orchestra as I was. To Benny, performing with the BSO had become a mundane job.

We were playing Tchaikovsky's *Pathétique* Symphony, a great favorite of Koussevitzky's. In fact, he never allowed any guest conductor to program it. Whenever we played it, the finale always brought a tear to Koussey's eye as he undoubtedly remembered his Mother Russia.

Near the end of this long symphony, the violins stop playing as the lower strings bring the symphony to a quiet and poignant close. At the rehearsal, Koussey admonished us to sit motionless with our violins on our knees as the symphony came to an end. There was a dramatic hush in the air of Symphony Hall, an almost eerie stillness. While I sat there looking down at the floor, deeply moved by the tragic music, Benny leaned over and whispered, "Bixsen, you like my new shoes?"

At one performance we were playing the long and physically exhausting Schubert Ninth Symphony, known as the "Great C Major." The last movement seems to go on forever, and is espe-

The Life of a Musician

cially tiring for the violins. Each time we turned a page, I heard Joe Leibovici behind me grunt: "Oy!" and at the end, "Damn Schubert! He wrote two symphonies, one unfinished and the other endless!"

Joe was a formidable violinist who came to the orchestra from his native Romania by way of Paris. He was not a happy man. Joe used to say, "I'm too good to play in the Boston Symphony, but not good enough to be a soloist." He criticized everybody and everything. No new composition was ever to Joe's liking. Under Koussevitzky we played a great deal of Aaron Copland's music, all of which sounded the same to Leibovici. After our first read-through of *Appalachian Spring*, Joe passed judgment. "I see Copland has composed a new title."

Every orchestra musician has a pet frustration, and each would like to be something or somebody else. One evening before a string quartet concert, our former solo violist, the late Jean Le-Franc, was furiously pacing up and down the green room, muttering to himself while he practiced. "You know, Dickson," he said to me, "I have played perhaps five, six thousand concerts in my life. All the time I am nervous! Better to be a plumbair."

Each musician is deeply concerned with his own technical problems, and each envies the other. There is probably not one oboe player in the whole world who is satisfied with his lot; not a horn player who doesn't look forward eagerly to his retirement; not a string player who wouldn't rather play one of the "easy" wind instruments.

Yet it seems to me after many years of observation that, with few exceptions, certain characteristics go with certain instruments. It may be that these characteristics prompted the choice of instrument, or were acquired because of the instrument. Never-

Beating Time

theless they are there for all to notice. (In some of the following comments I take the liberty of plagiarizing my first book, *Gentlemen, More Dolce Please,* since it has long been out of print.)

The cellists are still the greatest source of trouble in an orchestra. They are prima donnas—supersensitive, suspicious, conceited, and quarrelsome. Among the dozen cellists in an orchestra, hardly any two speak to each other. When Koussevitzky first came to the Boston Symphony Orchestra with his reputation as a former bass virtuoso, the cellists looked upon him with disdain. After all, Arturo Toscanini was a cellist, and so was Sir John Barbirolli, both conductors—but a bass player? Shortly after his appointment, Koussey was asked by the members of the orchestra to play for them. After some hesitation and a bit of coaxing, he consented. One of the cellists later reported to his wife, "It was astounding. I have never heard such bass playing. I closed my eyes and said to myself, 'That is not a bass. It sounds like a lousy cello!'"

There was a time when the basses were the solid citizens of an orchestra. They did their job, giving no trouble and expecting no praise. Koussevitzky changed all that. Throughout the world now bass players have become almost as temperamental as cellists.

Viola players are usually the least troublesome. They are mostly ex-fiddlers who have become philosophical about their role of playing the deadly dull inner voice. A story is told about a viola player who dreamed he was playing Handel's *Messiah* and woke up to find he was. Viola players are the traditional victims of bad jokes:

"What do you do with a dead viola player?"

"You put him on the last stand."

"Why are viola players' fingers like lightning?"

"Because they never strike the same place twice."

The Life of a Musician

Viola players accept these pejorative remarks with detached good humor and don't even resent being looked down upon by their violinist colleagues as broken-down fiddlers. There was a time when the viola section of an orchestra was made up of the oldest players, and any violist under sixty was contemplated with great sympathy. "So young, and already a viola!" Modern performance standards, however, demand that the violist be on a par with the violinist, and today's professional players are genuine virtuosi.

The violins in an orchestra are traditionally divided into two sections, first and second, with a distinct difference in status between the two. Yet in a good orchestra there is no difference in the abilities of the players. A newcomer starts as a second violinist and eventually moves into the firsts, depending on the longevity of the latter. Yet in the mind of the public, there is a kind of stigma to "playing second fiddle." In reality the second violin part is just as essential to a composition as any other. (Years ago I overheard the end of an argument between a German triangle player and another colleague: "Mine part is just as prominenten like your'n.") Some day, I hope, we will do away with the term "second violin." Perhaps "mezzo-violin" would be a better term. Until then, the first violins will continue to be aristocrats, wrapped in an aura of superiority no matter how undeserved, while the seconds remain frustrated and unsung.

If oboists are slightly less troublesome than the cellists, it is only because there are fewer of them. Oboists are a breed unto themselves, the unhappiest of musicians, constantly complaining and bemoaning their fate at having to play such an unpredictable, treacherous instrument. Most of their time is spend endlessly fussing with their double reeds. Onstage, the oboist is the most fid-

Beating Time

gety member of the orchestra. Each time there is more than a bar's rest, the reed is removed, inspected, cursed, and put back just in time for the next entrance. Between movements, the reed is shaved with the blade that lies close to every oboe player.

In any orchestra, the flute players are the best dressed, the quietest, and the easiest to get along with. They play the least troublesome of all instruments—no reed problems, no mouthpiece trouble, no string problems—and consequently are the best-adjusted citizens of the symphony orchestra. The flute players are the happiest members and the most affluent. Everybody wants to take flute lessons!

Clarinetists are the classic complainers of every orchestra, looking down their noses at any kind of vibrato, which is part of the technique of almost every instrument but theirs. They are forever hunting for a good reed—which they never find.

Bassoon players are an affable lot. They, like the oboists, play a double-reed instrument, but it seems to affect them differently. The bassoonist is as sweet as the oboist is sour. Many of the bassoon players I have known were involved in myriad outside activities—telescope making, flying, skiing, bow making, organ building. Every bassoon player is a handyman and usually highly intelligent.

Most trumpet players are debonair and dashing. Even when they grow old and gray, they retain a certain air of charm. Trumpet players are usually bon vivants with a taste for good wine and pretty women. (Female trumpeters, though no longer rare, have not yet become part of the BSO.)

Trombone players, on the other hand, are more like ministers. Usually quiet and highly moral, in my day they were the good, solid citizens of the orchestra, never complaining, going about

The Life of a Musician

their business quietly and efficiently. Nobody ever heard of a rebellious trombone player.

If trombonists are ministerial, horn players are definitely not. The most dissatisfied of all musicians, constantly agitating for more pay and less work, horn players have been able to convince conductors that their lips can stand only so much playing, and most symphony orchestras have double platoons. It is practically unheard of that one horn player should play an entire concert.

There is only one tuba player in the entire orchestra, and he enjoys a certain amount of prestige—and loneliness. Tuba players never talk. They are silent, morose, and uncommunicative. They do sing to themselves, usually in a high register. Tuba players have no common interests with any of their fellow musicians and usually strike up a friendship with the stage manager. How does one get to be a tuba player? Mostly by accident: someone willed a tuba to the family, the high school orchestra needed one, the local town band was without a tuba player, or some other reason. Yet the present-day orchestral tuba player is a consummate artist. The player in the Boston Symphony does the most amazing things on his unwieldy instrument, including playing all the French horn concertos, for which he does not endear himself to his horn colleagues.

The male percussion players—and men are still a large majority here—are the strong, virile he-men of any orchestra. If the orchestra were ever physically threatened, the percussionists would be our front line of defense. Since percussionists play many instruments, they are jacks of all trades, constantly fixing and building. Percussionists can repair anything from a tambourine to a violin to an automobile.

The timpanist is the grand potentate of the percussionists, and he almost never deigns to play anything but his soup kettles. During a performance, while his underlings scurry back and forth from triangle to snare to block to xylophone to cymbal, the timpanist presides quietly and benignly over his calfskins (or the modern-day nylon equivalent), mallet in each hand, proudly surveying his domain.

If musicians have mental and emotional characteristics that go with their instruments, they also have readily identifiable physical scars. If the dead body of a musician were found, a little detective work would reveal the instrument he or she played. The calluses on the fingers of the left hand mark every string player. Violinists would also have a mark on the left side of the neck, the viola player a slightly larger mark. Cellists could be identified by the calluses on their left fingers plus one on the left thumb; they are the only string players who use the thumb. They would also have a red mark on the chest where the cello presses against the body. A string bass player would have larger calluses, and the jazz bassist would, in addition, have calluses on his right hand, the result of slapping the strings.

Clarinetists have, on the inside of the right thumb, their own brand of callus, the result of years of supporting their instrument. The unmistakable battle scars of the harpist are calluses on only eight fingers. The little fingers are never used in playing the harp. An exception was Harpo Marx, who was largely self-taught. Harpo once came to Bernard Zighera, the BSO's distinguished harpist, for lessons. Zighera was so flabbergasted at the completely unorthodox way that Marx played—and so well—that he told Marx he couldn't teach him anything.

What of left-handed violinists? I know of only two, although there may be others. Rudolph Kolisch, who taught at the New

The Life of a Musician

England Conservatory and founded the Kolisch String Quartet, was a fine violinist who learned to play holding the violin in his right hand because of an accident to two fingers of his left hand. Another left-handed violinist was Charlie Chaplin, and why he played that way I don't know. Actually, even if a person is born left-handed, he or she can learn to play the violin normally, because at the beginning a student is equally awkward with either hand. The great former concertmaster of the BSO, now conductor of the Utah Symphony, Joseph Silverstein, happens to be left-handed but trained to play right-handed.

One of the unsung heroes of every symphony orchestra is its librarian, who is responsible for every piece of music on each stand. It is the unfortunate librarian who is openly chastised by the musicians—and especially the conductor—if any instrumental part is missing or out of place. The librarian spends countless hours long before rehearsals begin, ordering new music, organizing the parts and the conductor's score, copying bowings in the string parts, and inserting cuts and special directions.

Leslie Rogers enjoyed the longest tenure of any of the BSO librarians. His whole life was the Boston Symphony library, and he possessed an uncanny memory for details. He knew by heart the catalog number of almost every score in the vast library and could quote the length of each movement, the dates of its prior performances, and the conductor who led the orchestra. Leslie served the BSO from 1912 to 1956, when he died in Munich while the orchestra was on tour. It was he who catalogued the entire library of thousands of scores into a system still used today.

Leslie was succeeded by my old friend and colleague Victor Alpert, an excellent musician who reluctantly gave up his viola to become chief librarian of the BSO. Victor served from 1956 to

Beating Time

1984, when he returned to his first love, performing. He remains a good friend and my private librarian, whose wealth of knowledge I am constantly tapping.

Since 1984 the BSO has had as its librarian Martin Burlingame, an urbane, witty, affable fount of musical knowledge. There is hardly anything about music that Marty doesn't know or isn't willing to share.

Unlike classical musicians of the past, today's players are by no means one-dimensional, but develop many other interests and hobbies in addition to their principal craft. When I was with the BSO, two of the violinists had been amateur boxers. Another was an expert auto mechanic, and another a former competitive speed skater. The bassoonist Ernst Panenka, Viennese by birth, was an amateur astronomer who spent years building his own telescope; on moonlit nights when we were not playing, he would invite his colleagues to his roof to study the stars. The late Sherman Walt, our beloved first bassoonist, had been a fighter pilot in World War II and was an expert downhill skier. We had two licensed pilots in the orchestra who flew their own planes—Joe Hearne and Wayne Rapier. Sheldon Rotenberg, a violinist and former captain in army intelligence in World War II, was an expert tennis player and for a while coached the tennis team of his alma mater, Tufts University. Burton Fine, the first violist, held a couple of advanced degrees and was once employed by NASA in the development of America's space program.

Martin Hoherman, a former assistant first cellist, came to the United States from his native Poland by way of Singapore and Hong Kong after a stint in the British army. In addition to his abilities as an outstanding cellist, Hoherman played nine or ten other instruments and was occasionally called upon to perform

The Life of a Musician

when needed as a pianist, banjoist, saxophonist, or what have you. Name an instrument, Martin Hoherman could play it. If he couldn't, give him a few hours' practice time! He also repaired watches. The late Karl Zeise, another fine cellist and expert amateur painter, used to arrange the exhibits in the Symphony Hall art gallery.

Pat Cardillo was the great chef of the Boston Symphony. His culinary skills were such that an invitation to one of his meals was eagerly sought by all his colleagues. There used to be a fierce rivalry between Cardillo and another great cook, Joe DePasquale, and for years I received free meals by acting as a referee. I would be invited first to one house, then to the other, and would pronounce each meal the best I had ever eaten.

The bassoonist Matthew Ruggiero used to repair violins and bows. What started as a hobby to help his wife, a fine violinist, quickly became a convenience for the violinists of the orchestra, until it turned into such a time-consuming side occupation that he finally had to give it up. In his spare time Matthew also earned a Ph.D. in Italian literature from Harvard. Richard Plaster, a contrabassoonist, built organs and clavichords in his spare time. Everett Firth, the BSO's timpanist, is an art collector and has a sizable collection of nineteenth- and twentieth-century American paintings.

One would think that handling dangerous tools would be taboo for a musician, yet a number of my former colleagues were quite expert at using them. The late violinist Noah Bielski, who played at Carnegie Hall at age seven, used to spend hours in his home workshop surrounded by various woodworking tools, including a set of electric saws.

The day is past when musicians were dreamers and not ex-

pected to know anything of the practical sciences. Charles Kavalovski, the BSO's admirable first horn, holds a Ph.D. in experimen-
tal nuclear physics and was once a professor at Washington State
University.

Perhaps the most unusual second career in the orchestra was
that of Bill Marshall, who played on the first stand of second violins. Reverend William Marshall was an ordained Pentecostal minister. I wonder if any other orchestra in the world can claim a
member of the clergy among its personnel.

Life in a symphony orchestra is hard, exacting, and emotional,
yet stimulating and rewarding. Playing in the BSO is generally a
lifetime affair. Musicians gripe constantly, yet almost no one ever
wants to leave. Players keep saying "one more year" until, in some
cases, they are nearly eighty, as I was when I retired. There are
the inevitable exceptions, however. We had a bassoon player, Raymond Allard, who retired in his middle fifties. He was a marvelous
player who claimed he hated music; when he left the orchestra,
he vowed he would never touch the instrument again except to
plant flowers in it—which he did. There was a horn player, Marcel Lannoye, whose ambition was to throw his horn under the
wheels of Koussevitzky's car and calmly walk off to his retirement.
I once overheard the following conversation between two Russian
violinists: "Nicolai, I would like to retire. Vot should I do?" "Just
play for the conductor!"

Joseph DePasquale, our first violist, and Samuel Mayes, our first
cellist, were lured away from the BSO by Eugene Ormandy, not
only to play in the Philadelphia Orchestra, but also to teach at
the Curtis Institute of Music. Despite an occasional defection,
though, the majority of players in the BSO stay throughout their
careers, which extend in some cases to a ripe old age. One of

The Life of a Musician

the orchestra's violinists, Samuel Diamond, went home after an evening rehearsal and died peacefully in his sleep after fifty years with the BSO. Rolland Tapley, a violinist, retired after a record-breaking fifty-seven years with the Boston Symphony.

Today there is no mandatory retirement age in the Boston Symphony, nor in any other major orchestra. William Kincaid, one of the great flutists of our time, had been forced to retire from the Philadelphia Orchestra while still playing beautifully, only because he had reached the retirement age of sixty-five. John Corigliano, the admirable concertmaster of the New York Philharmonic, also had to leave when he reached sixty-five (a very young and still enormously capable sixty-five), only to be welcomed as concertmaster of the San Antonio Symphony Orchestra.

When I joined the BSO in 1938 as one of its youngest members, the average age of the players was a good deal higher than it is today. More older members have gradually retired, so that today the average age is lower. Perhaps the biggest change is the number of women in the orchestra: about one-fifth of the personnel, most of whom have joined in the past twenty years.

After a lifetime in music I retain a special admiration for my player colleagues, whose talents never cease to amaze me.

11

Conductors

౿ The cellist Gregor Piatigorsky had a cynical view of conductors. "They are a necessary evil," he would say, "but they should be hidden from the view of the audience, perhaps behind a screen. When I go to a play, I don't see the director telling the actors what to say. Why should I be subjected to a conductor? I have played with many conductors, tall ones, short ones, fat ones, thin ones. They all have one thing in common: not one suffers from an inferiority complex!"

The art of conducting is relatively new in the history of music. Until the nineteenth century it did not exist. Bach and Handel led their music from their seats at the harpsichord or organ. The seventeenth-century French composer Lully, while beating time on the floor with his long "beating stick," accidentally punctured his toe and died of blood poisoning. When Louis Spohr came to London in 1820 with a small orchestra, he astounded the audience as well as the critics by leading his players with a baton. Since then the role of conductors has become all-important. Indeed, from a purely practical role theirs has evolved into one of glamour and prestige.

How are conductors chosen? Strangely enough, the opinions

Beating Time

of musicians have seldom mattered. In its century-old existence, the Boston Symphony Orchestra has had thirteen conductors. Not one was chosen by the musicians. They were chosen sometimes by the manager, sometimes by only one or two members of the board of trustees.

A number of years ago, when the San Francisco Orchestra was seeking a new conductor, the trustees decided that after a season of guest conductors, they would ask the musicians to choose. That conductor turned out to be a disaster. On the other hand, when the Cleveland Orchestra lost George Szell, the trustees engaged a series of conductors for one season, and after having solicited the players' opinions, hired the extremely talented Lorin Maazel, who had received only two votes. Subsequently, Maazel received the following telegram from Erich Leinsdorf, a candidate not chosen: "Congratulations! Suggest you find the two who voted for you and fire them to create unanimity in the orchestra."

Orchestra players have a strange relationship with conductors. They usually hate them. The favorite pastime of musicians in the tuning room is belittling the conductor. Musicians are notorious cynics, and no conductor enjoys a "honeymoon" with his orchestra longer than a couple of years. But it doesn't really matter. Professional musicians have an innate pride in playing their best, no matter who is conducting.

The behavior of conductors has changed considerably since the days of the "big three": Koussevitzky, Toscanini, and Stokowski. Conductors in those days were tyrannical, unpredictable megalomaniacs, and those who hired them expected them to be.

Toscanini's uncontrollable outbursts at rehearsals were expected and even tolerated because of the players' respect for him as a musician. Toscanini once threw his baton at a violinist, almost

Conductors

blinding him. On his birthday at a rehearsal with the NBC orchestra, Toscanini was presented with an expensive gold watch. During the rehearsal nothing could please him, and he kept getting angrier and angrier. Finally he took the new watch out of his pocket, slammed it on floor, and stomped out. The orchestra manager scooped up the pieces and had the watch repaired. A few weeks later he presented Toscanini with a box containing two watches—the repaired one and an inexpensive Ingersoll, under which was a note: "For rehearsals only." Toscanini was not amused.

Toscanini seemed never to be satisfied, either at concerts or at rehearsals, and there was always a pained expression on his face. His favorite (and constant) reprimand was, "Vergogna!" and one day he stopped to explain: "Vergogna! You know what that means? It means 'shame!'" After Toscanini had been in the United States for a number of years, he went back to Italy for a performance with La Scala. At his first rehearsal with the orchestra, he shouted, "Shame! You know what that means? It means 'vergogna!'"

Serge Koussevitzky was a tough taskmaster—temperamental, unreasonable, and unpredictable. Yet he never fired anyone. He considered the players his children, and indeed often addressed them at rehearsals as "Kinder." There were a few instances when there was trouble, like the time when Jean Bedetti, our first cellist, walked out during a rehearsal. It was a Thursday morning, the final rehearsal for the weekend concerts, and visitors were in the hall, allowed by Koussevitzky to attend. That day Koussey was particularly nasty to the players and began to criticize Bedetti's short solo. "No! Too fast. No! Too loud. No! It is out of tune!" Finally, Bedetti picked up his cello and walked off the stage mumbling, "Get someone else to play." Koussevitzky was livid and announced to the orchestra, "This man will never come back." After a week of absence, and presumably an apology, Bedetti returned, and nothing more was said of the incident.

There was another incident with Gaston Dufresne, one of the Boston Symphony's fine bass players, whom Koussevitzky accused of "sleeping." "I do not sleep," Dufresne shouted back, and of course was asked to leave. After two weeks, and another presumed apology, Dufresne was also back in the orchestra.

During the early 1940s, while I was comparatively new in the orchestra, I learned to my chagrin of Koussevitzky's lack of humor. My colleagues and I put together an evening of fun, a kind of vaudeville show that would feature the "hidden talents" of the members of the BSO. It took place in the ballroom of a downtown hotel before an audience of contributors to our pension fund. Some of the acts were bizarre. Richard Burgin, our concertmaster, performing as Dick Burgin and His Hep-Cats, conducted a small group of his long-hair colleagues in a short jazz concert. Einar Hansen, a violinist and physical culture expert, did a Russian dance. Georges Mager, our first trumpeter with a surprisingly good tenor voice, rendered a duet with his wife, an equally good soprano. Emil Kornsand, a violinist, did magic tricks, and so it went all evening. Koussevitzky, sitting in the audience, seemed to be enjoying the antics of his "kinder" until an uncalculated mishap.

Jacobus Langendoen, our associate first cellist, and I had written a short sketch that we thought would be funny. It took place in a barbershop where "Langendoni" was the barber and I, "Dickasoni," a Boston Symphony musician, came in for a shave. I rushed into the shop and said: "I need a quick shave. I have a concert."

"Where do you play?" asked the barber.

"Boston Symphony," I replied.

"Who's the conductor?" he asked.

Conductors

I replied, "I don't know. Somebody's waving a stick, but I don't look. I mind my own business."

Six months later, at a concert in Sanders Theater, Koussey walked by me as he left the stage and whispered: "Even if you don't know who is the conductor, you must watch!" About a year later, at a difficult rehearsal when Koussey was especially disagreeable, he blurted out: "It is not together! How can it be together when a gentleman not know who is the conductor?"

From then on I made it my business never to take my eyes off Koussey. That didn't help. One day he suddenly stopped in the middle of a familiar Haydn symphony and said: "When we are playing a symphony that you know and I know, it is not necessary to look always at the conductor!"

I remember a rehearsal in the pre-union era when Koussey noticed a musician looking at his watch. He furiously stretched out the rehearsal a half hour longer, threatening, in his colorful English, "Ve vill rehearse tousand times over again until ve vill not have dat vot it need!" After unionization, that began to change. No longer, except on rare occasions, were rehearsals extended beyond their scheduled duration. Although he himself had advocated unionization, its constraints bothered him. At one rehearsal he blurted out: "Since you join union, you play like employers!" (He meant "employees.")

In my half century with the Boston Symphony, I have played under five permanent conductors and many guest conductors, and each one had his own special quality.

Serge Koussevitzky had the power of establishing a personal relationship with each member of the orchestra. He made you feel that he was conducting you alone. After each performance, we felt as emotionally drained as he. Koussey's great concern was for

Beating Time

beauty of sound; his constant admonition, "More dolce!," produced a tonal quality in the Boston Symphony admired by audiences and critics to this day. Koussevitzky's approach to music was
a personal one. He embraced each piece of music, old or new, as
his own and paid scant attention to the composer's markings. Fast
movements were sometimes taken at tremendously exaggerated,
virtuosic speed, while slow movements were stretched out to the
limit. We were once rehearsing the slow movement of the *Eroica*,
and it kept getting slower and slower. Koussey suddenly stopped
and said, "I know the critics will say it is too slow, but when it is
so beautiful, I cannot let go."

After Koussevitzky's twenty-five years with the Boston Symphony Orchestra, Charles Munch began his thirteen years as music director. The difference in the personalities and musical habits
of these two men was evident. Koussey rehearsed everything
down to its smallest detail, and performances never varied from
what was decided at rehearsal. Munch, on the other hand, was a
great rhapsodist, and no two performances were alike. He once
said, "Any conductor who knows the exact tempo of a piece before he begins is a machine."

It was great fun playing under Munch. Some performances,
such as Berlioz's *Symphonie Fantastique* or Debussy's *La Mer*, were exciting, while some concerts were near catastrophes. At a performance in Washington, D.C., of Beethoven's Seventh Symphony,
Munch began conducting the first movement at such a slow tempo
that our first oboist, Fernand Gillet, assumed it was in two rather
than four, and by the time we reached the sixth bar, half the orchestra was playing in two, half in four. There was a feeling of
panic; Munch waved the orchestra to stop, and we started again.
Not a word of this was mentioned in the reviews the next day.

Conductors

After Munch came the era of the cerebral, methodical, coldly aloof Erich Leinsdorf. Unlike Munch, Leinsdorf carefully analyzed and worked out every piece of music before rehearsal. His relationship with the players was that of an executive, impersonally assigning responsibility. He spoke only to the first players, holding them responsible for their sections. "Mr. Kavalovski, the horns are out of tune; please see to it. Mr. Silverstein, the violins are not together." The rest of us resented it, yet we had great respect for Leinsdorf's knowledge and experience and played fine, technically exacting performances with him.

William Steinberg's few years with the orchestra were marked by uncertainty. He was not well, and one was never sure of his being able to appear onstage. The concerts he did conduct, however, especially Mahler, Bruckner, Mozart, and Beethoven, were wonderfully satisfying, like old wine. It was because of Steinberg's illness that Michael Tilson Thomas was given his chance. During the intermission of a Carnegie Hall concert, Steinberg came offstage and announced to the assistant conductor, "You're on, Michael; I cannot continue." Michael quickly changed into his evening clothes and waited in the wings while our manager, Tod Perry, announced to the audience the sudden illness of Maestro Steinberg and his replacement by Tilson Thomas. Thus began the brilliant career of Michael Tilson Thomas.

As a successor to William Steinberg, the Boston Symphony Orchestra now has the dynamic Seiji Ozawa, the most naturally endowed conductor I have ever known. I have yet to see him make an awkward move. His conducting gestures are so natural and musically interpretive that there is never any doubt as to their meaning. Added to his beautiful grace and dynamism are a fine musical sense, complete knowledge of the score, and an uncanny mem-

Beating Time

ory—Ozawa conducts entire operas by heart. What is remarkable about Ozawa is that, having been brought up in his native Japan, he never heard a live concert by a symphony orchestra until he was in his middle teens.

With Seiji, rehearsals have become less formal. Everyone is on a first-name basis, even he, and he has endeavored to instill a democratic spirit in the orchestra by inviting suggestions and comments from the musicians. If that works in the long run, I will have to change my conviction that an orchestra must be a benign dictatorship. Although Seiji invites the opinions of others, he finds it difficult to agree with them. At auditions for orchestra vacancies, Ozawa often disagrees even with the unanimous consensus of the orchestra committee, and vacancies remain unfilled for long periods of time. At every concert and rehearsal, there are numerous substitutes. Some of these players have substituted with the orchestra for years, while Seiji has yet to make up his mind whether to offer a permanent position. Like Koussevitzky, Ozawa has also been known to promise a promotion to a player, then change his mind. (Koussey once explained his vagaries thus: "I know I have the weakness to make promises, but I have the strength not to keep the promise.")

My own conducting began years ago, when at age fourteen I led Grace Hushen and Her Melody Boys. In the ensuing years I conducted a number of community orchestras. In the summer of 1955, at my wife's urging, and to evaluate where I stood with other conductors, I attended the conducting school of the eminent Pierre Monteux in Hancock, Maine. Monteux had preceded Koussevitzky as conductor of the BSO and served from 1919 to 1924. This was the first of a number of summers I would spend

Conductors

there, and over the years I valued my association and friendship with that gentle philosopher-musician.

I have never believed that conducting can be taught. Who were the teachers of Toscanini, Koussevitzky, and Stokowski? I attended the school primarily to evaluate myself, to find out how I stacked up against other conductors, many of them well established and well known. The physical aspects of conducting were never discussed at the Monteux school. It was assumed that everyone knew how to beat the standard time signatures. Only the music, and how best to perform it, was of importance, and here is where Monteux's wealth of experience was so valuable. His main points of discussion were those of tempo, balance, and intonation. Monteux's advice to conductors as they stood before the orchestra was practical as well as instructional. "Don't talk too much," he would advise; "they will not listen." Once he even admitted, "A good conductor knows when to follow the orchestra."

Pierre Monteux was a dear, kind, simple man. Short and round, he had a rotund figure and jet-black hair, with a contrasting gray walrus mustache. Once, accused of dyeing his hair, Pierre publicly announced a ten-thousand-dollar prize to anyone able to wash out the black color. He was always calm; nothing seemed to ruffle him, not even his irrepressible third wife, Doris, a Maine Yankee whom he adored and referred to as his "Eroica." Doris once burst into the hall during a class and shouted, "Pierre, I'm leaving you and never coming back!" There was silence in the room as Monteux slowly rose from his seat. "Leave the checkbook," he said.

The final concert at the end of the season at Hancock was a gala affair. The hall was packed with neighboring townspeople, with the overflow on the lawn. The Monteuxs sat in the front row

Beating Time

to one side while his students conducted. There were no programs. Mrs. Monteux announced each piece in her Yankee drawl, and often got them wrong. Once she announced, "The overture to *Der Freischutz* by Beethoven"; Monteux calmly got up and loudly proclaimed, "She means Weber!"

At the end of the summer session, Monteux asked if there was anything he could do for me. I told him that I would like to study the opera *Carmen* with him. He agreed, and I spent a whole day with him and a pianist going over every note of the score. When it was over he presented me with his own score, which he autographed with the inscription: "To my friend Harry Dickson, with my true affection, Pierre Monteux."

One of my most memorable concerts was the one conducted by Pierre Monteux on April 4, 1955. It was the 119th pension fund concert of the BSO and celebrated Monteux's eightieth birthday. It was an all-Beethoven program with Pierre's good friend Leon Fleischer playing Beethoven's Fourth Piano Concerto.

Some months before the concert, I spoke with Charles Munch about asking Igor Stravinsky and Darius Milhaud, both composers having had a long association with Monteux, to write special pieces for the occasion. With Munch's permission, I wrote to Stravinsky and Milhaud. A piece for strings, "Pensées amicales pour mon ami, Pierre Monteux," arrived from Milhaud, and much later, a few days before the concert, a "Birthday Prelude to Pierre Monteux" came from Stravinsky's publisher, Boosey and Hawkes, with a bill for performance. Leslie Rogers, our librarian, was so incensed at getting the bill that he called the publishers and shamed them into waiving the performance fee.

The concert was unforgettable. Symphony Hall was festooned

Conductors

with a garland of roses spelling out the number "80" over the orchestra. After intermission there was a speech by the president of the trustees, Henry Cabot. Then, as Monteux sat by the podium, Charles Munch conducted the two pieces especially written in Monteux's honor. The concert ended with Beethoven's *Eroica*.

After the concert there was a party at a local hotel, which I had arranged. Seated at the head table with the Monteuxs were the African-American tenor Roland Hayes; "Doc" Davison, the conductor of the Harvard Glee Club; and BSO concertmaster Richard Burgin. The lives of all of these people had been influenced by Pierre Monteux while he was conductor of the Boston Symphony Orchestra. Hayes spoke movingly: "It was Pierre Monteux who made me the first of my race to appear with a symphony orchestra." Davison thanked Monteux for introducing the Harvard Glee Club in Boston Symphony performances, and Burgin expressed his appreciation to Monteux for having chosen him as concertmaster.

After the dinner there was a short concert by a dozen musicians of the orchestra, those players who had been engaged when Monteux was the conductor years ago. Jacobus Langendoen had composed a sort of musical biography of Monteux. I narrated as the music was played. The piece began with a Kreutzer étude, a reference to Monteux's musical beginnings as a violinist. There were excerpts from Stravinsky's *Rite of Spring*, which Monteux had premiered, interspersed with his favorite Strauss waltz, "Voices of Spring." Each section of the piece ended in "Happy Birthday."

Knowing that Monteux had composed in his youth, I had conspired with his wife, who sent me a piece of music hidden away in a closet, a string composition he had written at the age of eigh-

Beating Time

teen. Before we played it, I announced that we had found an old piece of music by an unknown composer and would like the *maître* to identify it for us. When we had played just a few bars, Monteux turned to his wife. "Where did zey get zat?" he asked. The composition was quite sentimental, and when we finished, Monteux announced, "I think the composer should remain anonymous."

The fully outfitted Melody Boy, Harry Ellis Dickson, strikes a pose with his violin around 1922.

Grace Hushen poses with her Melody Boys in the early twenties. A bespectacled Harry Ellis Dickson sits to her left.

A twenty-five-year-old Harry Ellis Dickson poses with his parents, Ellis and Ethel Dickson, about 1934.

Harry Ellis Dickson plays solo during an early (1941) Boston Symphony Orchestra tour stop. Audiences tended to be larger when the entire orchestra performed.

Always the ladies' man, Harry is surrounded here by his wife, Jane, and two daughters, Kitty and Jinny.

Photographed in Hancock, Maine, in 1955 are, from left to right, Harry Ellis Dickson, Pierre Monteux, and Charles Brook.

From left to right, Arthur Fiedler, Thomas Perry, and Harry Ellis Dickson talk with the French consul after Harry received an award in L'Ordre des Arts et des Lettres.

Harry Ellis Dickson grabs Arthur Fiedler at the Berlin wall, lest he consider any means of securing a tour of East Germany for the Boston Pops.

Harry Ellis Dickson and daughter Kitty greet good friend Danny Kaye at Boston's Logan Airport in 1965.

A dapper Harry Ellis Dickson is flanked in this 1976 photo by daughters Kitty (his right) and Jinny (his left).

Harry Ellis Dickson arm in arm with Joel Grey.

A jubilant Harry Ellis Dickson acknowledges applause after his final BSO concert, in 1987. Seiji Ozawa stands to Harry's right in the Shed at Tanglewood. Photo by Walter Scott.

Harry Ellis Dickson introduces flutist James Galway to the presidential candidate and his wife, Michael and Kitty Dukakis, after a 1987 Boston Symphony concert. Photo courtesy of Lincoln Russell.

The camera captures, from left to right, Michael Dukakis, Joan Kennedy, and the tuxedoed duo of Harry Ellis Dickson and John Williams.

Sharing a moment of glory at the 1988 Democratic National Convention in Atlanta are, from left to right, John and Lisa Dukakis, Euterpe Dukakis, Harry Ellis Dickson, and Michael and Kitty Dukakis. Behind Michael and Kitty are Mr. and Mrs. Lloyd Bentsen.

Harry Ellis Dickson relaxes at the park named in his honor in 1991. The park is conveniently located around the corner from Symphony Hall. Photo courtesy of Lincoln Russell.

The Maestro feeds the body as well as the soul: a youngster accepts cake offered by Harry Ellis Dickson at a Youth Concerts party.

Harry Ellis Dickson poses with the perennially popular local television personalities Natalie Jacobson and Chet Curtis at a 1993 Salute to Symphony.

Harry Ellis Dickson displays his conducting prowess during a Boston Pops matinee performance.

12

Guest Conductors

↶ Of all the guest conductors who performed during my years in the BSO, certain ones stand out. During the eleven years of Sir Colin Davis's tenure as principal guest conductor, there were many concerts of wonderful music making. I have never known a conductor who loved music as did Sir Colin Davis, an affection he was able to instill in all of us.

Sir John Barbirolli brought a sense of camaraderie to the orchestra. He treated the players as friends and fellow musicians—he himself had been a cellist in an orchestra. I remember at one rehearsal his going into the cello section, borrowing Jean Bedetti's instrument, and demonstrating a certain passage, to the applause of the orchestra. "Do not applaud," he said; "I am out of practice."

When Sir Thomas Beecham came to conduct, there were no absences in the orchestra. Even if people were sick, they came to rehearsal so as not to miss the witty remarks of Sir Thomas. I was never quite convinced of the thoroughness of his musical training, but rather thought of him as a charming dilettante. During rehearsals Sir Thomas kept up a constant patter of remarks. After an oboe passage in a Sibelius symphony, he shouted, "Bravo! Beautifully played. But why didn't Sibelius give that to the clarinet?"

Beating Time

Sir Thomas never seemed to understand when someone asked a question. "Would you kindly speak English?" he would say; "I don't understand American." (A story went around the orchestra that Sir Thomas received a telephone call one morning in his room at the Ritz. A man with a pronounced Texas accent introduced himself. "Sir Thomas? Ah'm the president of thuh English-Speakin' Union." To which Sir Thomas replied, "I don't believe you," and hung up.) At one concert, the audience applauded before the final movement of a Handel piece. "Ladies and gentlemen," Sir Thomas admonished, "you evidently think the piece is over. I regret to inform you that it is not." Beecham told the audience that when he was a young conductor and came out for a bow after a concert, an elderly vicar sitting in the front row was heard to say: "Why do they applaud him? The musicians did all the work."

Bruno Walter was a dear, kind man who exuded music. He was one of the old masters, an embodiment of the term *maestro*. I remember especially his wonderful interpretations of Mozart and of Mahler, the latter a composer whom Walter knew.

The late Fritz Reiner, a first-rate conductor, was not especially endeared to his musicians. A Hungarian by birth, Reiner came to America in 1922 to conduct the Cincinnati Symphony, a post he held for nine years. Later he took over, in turn, the orchestra at the Curtis Institute, the Pittsburgh Symphony, and the Chicago Symphony. During all that time Reiner developed a reputation as a tough taskmaster, a formidable ogre. In each orchestra that he conducted, Reiner tried to fire half the personnel. At his own funeral, it was said among musicians, he fired three of his pallbearers! When during the 1945–46 season it was announced that Fritz Reiner was coming to conduct the BSO, there was a meeting

Guest Conductors

in the tuning room where the players decided that they would not take it from this devilish man. At the first rehearsal we waited for the expected venomous outburst. The piece was the Strauss *Domestic* Symphony. Reiner sat on his high stool, his glasses on the tip of his nose. For fifteen minutes, as he conducted, he did not utter a word. Then he stopped, peered over his glasses, and said, "Gentlemen, I am enjoying myself immensely!" For the entire week he was charming.

When we were told in 1943 that one of our guest conductors would be André Kostelanetz, some eyebrows were raised. Kostelanetz, the conductor of the CBS Coca-Cola Hour, turned out to be one of the most sensational guests of the season. Born and trained in St. Petersburg, Russia, Kostelanetz, who was married to the famous soprano Lily Pons, came as a young man to this country, where he became famous for his semiclassical radio programs. I was astounded, as we all were, by his musical knowledge and his professionalism.

I once asked him after a concert: "Maestro, why don't you have a symphony orchestra?"

"Get me one and I'll quit Coca-Cola," he answered.

During the Koussevitzky years we had few guest conductors. Koussey was careful about inviting "safe" conductors, those who were not expected to make a big splash. Most of them were of the English variety; Sir Thomas Beecham, Sir Adrian Boult, Sir Eugene Goossens. The one big mistake that Koussey felt he had made was to invite the unknown Greek conductor Dimitri Mitropoulos. It was Mitropoulos's first appearance in the United States, and he caused a sensation both among the musicians and with the audience. He had a commanding presence and a phenomenal memory. He conducted not only the concerts but also the rehearsals without a score. With no notes in front of him, he would say, "Three bars before G," or, "Six after F," or, "At the *andantino*," seeming to have a photo of the score in his brain.

Mitropoulos even knew each person in the orchestra by name. "How do you do it?" I asked him. "Oh," he said, "I memorized them from a program while on the plane coming here." Mitropoulos's concerts were spectacular, and his success was especially painful to Koussevitzky, who seemed to take it as a personal affront. "Imagine it," he told Richard Burgin, our concertmaster, "no one ever heard of this man. And he has such success!"

I have recently been reflecting on conducting and conductors. I have read about them, I have played under many, and I have inadvertently left some out of my remembrances. The vast majority of them have earned my respect and admiration—some more so than others. When I am asked what conductors really do, I am at a loss in trying to explain, even though I myself have conducted many orchestras. There is a charisma, a certain metaphysical power, in some conductors that inspires the players to give their best. What they actually do, and how they do it, is a mystery. I once asked Leonard Bernstein what makes a great conductor. "I really don't know," was his response.

Orchestra players smile indulgently, if not cynically, when they read about Bernstein's Mahler or Koussevitzky's Tchaikovsky, when neither Bernstein nor Koussevitzky has produced a sound. I remember the hurt expressed by Alfred Zighera, one of the great cellists in the Boston Symphony Orchestra, after reading of a guest conductor's warm sound in the cellos. "It is our sound, not his!" he complained.

Today's conductors usually eschew the score, if not in rehearsals, certainly at concerts, and even though I know that it makes

Guest Conductors

no difference in the performance, I, as well as the audience, am impressed. Charles Munch called them "memory acrobats." I have conducted entire concerts from memory and I know how difficult it is, how time consuming to commit to memory various scores. Yet Seiji Ozawa does it week in and week out. I have observed him at first rehearsal reading a score, and conducting the next day without it. What astonishes me especially is his ability to conduct even concerto accompaniments without a score, and he does it with authority.

There are legendary stories about the uncanny knowledge of past conductors, all of which added to their fame and untouchability. A second bassoon player once came to Toscanini's room before a concert to inform him that the E-flat key was not functioning on his instrument. Toscanini thought for a moment, then said, "Not to worry, you have no E flats to play tonight."

Yes, there is a mystique about conductors and conducting. Since I no longer play in the orchestra, when I attend a concert I find myself watching the conductor with more objectivity. I am awed by what I see: Seiji, graceful, pleading, hair flying, body twisting, perspiring. "Today's symphony performance," Igor Stravinsky once pointed out, "is a visual as well as an aural experience."

The role of the conductor has been exalted by concertgoers and critics, less so by players. A number of years ago the great Pablo Casals turned in his cello for a baton. His first conducting attempts were with the orchestra in Madrid. A friend visiting the concertmaster of that orchestra asked: "What is Casals conducting tonight?"

"I don't know what he's conducting, but we're playing Brahms' Fourth."

Some time ago there appeared in the media an item about an

Beating Time

affluent business executive who conducted a performance of Mahler's Second Symphony. An ardent music lover, he became obsessed with this symphony, listening to every recording of it he could find and traveling to all parts of the world wherever the symphony was being played, until he finally "knew" every note of it. He took some conducting lessons, engaged a London orchestra, and not only performed it but made a recording, which received salutary reviews.

When the late Danny Kaye, who could not read music, first conducted a Boston Symphony Orchestra Pension Fund concert, one music critic wrote, "By any musical standards, Danny Kaye is a great conductor."

How a beloved comedian who lacked any musical training became a guest conductor of the BSO is a story that warrants its own chapter.

13

"Maestro" Danny Kaye

⌒ On a Friday afternoon in 1956, I came off the stage into the tuning room and ran into Danny Kaye. I had never met him but was a longtime admirer. Kaye was in Boston for a one-man show to begin the following Monday. I was on the pension fund committee for the Boston Symphony and had read about his recent appearance with the Philadelphia Orchestra in a gala pension fund concert, in which he had "conducted" the orchestra.

"Mr. Kaye," I asked, "when are you going to conduct our orchestra?"

"Any time you ask me," he replied.

I ushered him up to Charles Munch's room. "Ah, Danny Kaye!" Munch exclaimed.

"Maître," I said, "we must have him conduct a pension fund concert."

Munch replied, "Certainement!"

At this point Tod Perry, the manager of the BSO, came into the room. We sat and talked, and by the time Danny had left, a concert had been arranged to take place three weeks thence, on a Thursday evening at 7:00 P.M. (Danny did not have to appear in his own show until after 9:30). In discussing the concert, Munch

Beating Time

said to Danny, "I will conduct the first piece—perhaps the Dukas *Apprenti Sorcier*—then you will take over." Danny agreed, and we walked out.

As we left Symphony Hall, Danny asked if I would drive him to his hotel. On the way he asked my name and who I was. Then he blurted out, "You've just got me in a hell of a lot of trouble! I've never conducted a whole concert! I know only one piece." He had learned Rossini's *La Gazza Ladra* Overture and had conducted it at the Philadelphia concert. "Will you help me?" Naturally, I agreed.

The next three weeks were hectic. Danny had a stereo brought into his hotel room and a number of recordings sent to him from his vast collection in Hollywood. I was with him a good part of every day as we planned a program. In spite of his not reading a note of music, he had an uncanny musical memory and perfect intonation. He could sing an entire symphony from beginning to end. As we listened to each recording, Danny made mental notes, never writing anything down. I was never quite sure how he was going to present each piece of music. I suggested he open the program with the Prelude to Act 3 of Wagner's *Lohengrin*. "Good," he said, "I've always wanted to conduct Wagner!" I went through the routine with him of how to beat different rhythms, most of which he already knew from having watched other conductors. Danny was a consummate master of mimicry and could reproduce anything he heard or saw. After going through a number of pieces, I insisted on writing them down to create some semblance of order in the program, a procedure that he thought quite unnecessary.

It is almost impossible to describe what went on at that first concert in Symphony Hall with Danny Kaye and the Boston Symphony Orchestra. Charles Munch conducted the Dukas piece, then took his place on the balcony overlooking the stage. Danny

"Maestro" Danny Kaye

entered, impeccably dressed in white tie and tails and carrying not one baton but a dozen. As the audience applauded, Danny bowed, then began a series of handshakes, first with the concertmaster, then with various players throughout the orchestra, stopping to kiss the few women. He then returned to the podium and began a ritual of choosing the right baton from the pile he had under his arm, discarding batons all over the stage. When he found the right one, he gave a downbeat to the orchestra, which responded with a loud B-flat major chord. Danny then turned around and shouted up to Munch, "Not bad, eh, Chuck?" He then broke off a piece of baton, gave another beat. This time the orchestra played a bit softer. Danny kept breaking off pieces of the baton, each time the chord becoming softer, until Danny held a baton about two inches long, and the chord was barely audible. Finally, with a one-inch baton, Danny made a tiny gesture; the orchestra exploded in the loudest chord of all. This was the beginning of the zaniest concert ever played by the BSO.

To illustrate an erratic conductor, in the middle of a phrase Danny would suddenly stop conducting, daring someone to play. Once our esteemed concertmaster, Richard Burgin, did play a note by himself. Danny fired him on the spot. When Burgin got up to leave, however, Danny followed him offstage, both of them returning arm in arm.

Danny conducted Rimsky-Korsakov's "Flight of the Bumblebee" with a flyswatter. In the Ravel *Bolero*, he conducted the first few bars, then walked offstage into the audience while the orchestra continued playing. He chatted with people, asked for a cigarette, and walked through the hall greeting members of the audience, returning to the stage in time to conduct the last four bars.

There was a piece on the program that Danny announced as a

Beating Time

"first performance by a composer imprisoned behind the Iron Curtain, who scratched the composition on the walls of the prison." The piece was simply made up as we went along, following Danny's direction to various sections of the orchestra. The wife of the famous cellist Emanuel Feuermann was in the audience and after the performance asked, "How could he memorize such a complicated piece?"

In the second part of the program, Danny conducted the finale of Beethoven's Fifth Symphony in a truncated version, which, I confess, was my doing, in order to show the audience that Beethoven wrote too many C major chords at the end. After the second of these chords, Danny turned around to bow, only to have the orchestra continue with more chords. Danny kept turning around after each chord, finally catching the last one.

After his concert with the BSO, Danny Kaye was besieged by other orchestras. I received permission to accompany him, and we did the circuit of all the major orchestras in the United States, plus some minor ones. Meanwhile, I assembled a library of his music, with annotations of some of his ridiculous changes. Whenever Danny had to conduct, the music was sent out from Symphony Hall. He refused any personal compensation, and succeeded in raising over ten million dollars for musicians' retirement funds. After a while, Danny became so enamored with his conducting skills that he almost became serious. Artur Rubinstein, Danny's friend, once said to me, "I am a little worried about him; I think he wants to do Beethoven's Ninth." Once, after a concert with the New York Philharmonic, Dimitri Mitropoulos scolded him. "A man with your talent should learn to read music." Danny shrugged Mitropoulos off, saying, "I'm afraid it would spoil me."

Danny Kaye had a remarkable talent for deflating pretense and

"Maestro" Danny Kaye

pomposity, and he was able to get away with it. His power of imitation was uncanny. When he was introduced at the first rehearsal of the New York Philharmonic by the manager, Bruno Zirato, who spoke in a pronounced Italian accent, Danny responded in exactly the same accent. After he had acknowledged the introduction, Danny said, "I understand you're a tough bunch. By the way, who's Gomberg? And who's Goodman?"—references to the first oboist and timpanist, respectively. "I understand you're the tough guys," he said, then launched into a profane tirade against them that convulsed the orchestra.

My friendship with Danny Kaye lasted thirty years, until his death in 1987, and it had a great influence on me and my family. I have never known anyone like him. He had an innate passion for humanity, and he constantly strove to understand and help others. Danny Kaye had a special love for and rapport with children everywhere, and they understood him no matter what language they spoke. He became the United Nations' ambassador for UNICEF and traveled all over the world, entertaining children with his special kind of humor and empathy.

My travels with Danny took me to Geneva, Rome, and Israel. In September 1967, shortly after the six-day Arab-Israeli War, Danny was invited to Israel to conduct the reorganized Gadna Orchestra, made up of young Israeli musicians serving in the army, many of whom had seen action in the recent war.

We boarded the 747 El-Al airplane in Rome, and immediately Danny and I were invited to sit in the cockpit with the flight crew. When we were about halfway to Tel Aviv, the chief pilot said, "Come on, Danny, take over." Danny had been flying a number of years and, amazingly enough, had been checked out to fly jet planes. Only in Israel, and only in the presence of Danny Kaye, could such a bizarre happening take place. Danny sat at the controls, guiding a planeful of people, all completely unaware that their chief pilot was "Captain" Danny Kaye.

As we approached Tel Aviv Danny turned to the chief pilot. "I guess you had better take over now."

"Anyone can fly a plane," the pilot answered, "let me see you land it." Danny made a perfect landing, to the applause of the other crew members. Then the pilot asked for his seat. "It will look strange," he said, "for you to be at the controls when we taxi in."

A crowd of dignitaries was waiting to greet Danny, but he excused himself and took me by the hand and led me outside. "I wanted you to see a real Jewish tree," he said, and then we returned to the waiting reception committee.

At the first rehearsal of the orchestra Danny was greeted warmly by the young musicians, some of whom had been wounded. Danny was especially concerned with the first cellist, whose arms and hands still showed the scars of war.

Danny took the orchestra on an Israel Bond tour of Europe and South America. After the concert in Geneva, before the orchestra departed for South America, I said good-bye to Danny.

"Well," he said, "I guess I don't need you anymore."

"Danny," I replied, "you never needed me," and I left for home and reality.

A person who regretted his lack of a college education, Danny tried to make up for it by delving into the arts and sciences with a great passion. He was a frustrated doctor and learned so much about medicine that he could discuss anatomy and surgery with physicians. He was one of the few laypersons allowed to stand by at operations performed by famous surgeons. Danny once even

"Maestro" Danny Kaye

diagnosed his own impending appendicitis attack, flew in his own plane to the Mayo Clinic, and "directed" his operation.

Danny Kaye was a social iconoclast who played upon human foibles. His sometimes outrageous treatment of others made them realize their own fallibility, and they accepted it with grace and good humor. Once I went with Danny to a meeting of the United Nations. We stood in the back behind a low wall, unseen by the members. Danny caught the eye of the president on the rostrum, a dignified South American diplomat, and began to wave at him with various hand signals. In a few minutes the president left the rostrum and the vice president took over. A woman tapped Danny on the shoulder and said, "Mr. Ambassador, the president would like to see you in his chambers." Danny asked me to come along, and when we entered the room the president scolded him. "Danny," he said, "you know this is very serious. You must not make fun here!"

Danny looked chagrined and asked, "Mr. President, did you leave the rostrum to see me or to go to the bathroom?"

The president burst into laughter and replied, "I cannot tell a lie. Both!"

Danny Kaye was a master at shocking people. When he was onstage he was circumspect, never uttering a word of profanity, but in private his language was colorful. During the first week of our friendship, he invited me and my wife and a few friends out to dinner. It was a startling experience for Jane, brought up as she had been in Europe and almost completely ignorant of American profanity. When we returned home she said to me, "I like Danny, but why does he use such language?" The next morning I was getting dressed to go to rehearsal and shouted down to Jane, who

Beating Time

was in the kitchen, to get me some underwear. "Get your own fucking underwear!" she shouted back. Later, whenever he called and Jane answered, Danny would ask her if she really had said it, and she would always deny it.

There were always incidents with Danny. I remember arriving in London with him around midnight. Just after we got to our hotel and settled in, there was a telephone call. I could hear him saying, "Yes ma'am. Don't worry, ma'am."

After he had hung up, I asked him, "Who was that?"

"Princess Margaret," he reported. "She was worried about my conducting." The next night Danny conducted the London Philharmonic, with his usual great success.

I played the innocent from Boston; Danny would introduce me to famous Hollywood people whom I pretended not to recognize. One day at the commissary at Paramount, where Danny was making a picture, he asked me if I knew the man at the next table. It was Robert Taylor, the handsome screen star. I knew Taylor was an amateur cellist who had taken lessons in Philadelphia from our first cellist of the BSO, Sam Mayes.

"Oh, sure," I said, "I know him. He's a cellist."

Danny looked at me quizzically, then motioned to Taylor to join us. We were introduced and Danny said, "Bob, I asked him if he knew you and he said you're a cellist!"

"I am," Taylor said. Danny looked at me and proceeded to recite a litany of his special profanity.

One evening while I was staying with Danny in California, he took me to a friend's house for dinner. When I asked him where we were going, he said, "You'll find out," and left it at that. We arrived at a spacious house with a long driveway, rang the bell,

"Maestro" Danny Kaye

and were shown in by a maid. I kept asking Danny where we were. "You'll find out," he repeated.

A woman came down the stairs, and before Danny could introduce me, she said, "Oh, you're Harry Dickson. Danny told me all about you." She looked familiar, but I really didn't recognize her. "My name is Shirley Parker," she said. I asked her what she did. "I'm a writer," she answered.

Before we sat down to dinner, I went to the bathroom, which was lined with Shirley MacLaine awards and testimonials. I suddenly realized whose house I was in. I came out and asked, "What do you have to do with Shirley MacLaine? Are you the president of her fan club?"

"Yes," she answered, "why do you ask?"

"Well," I said, "you've got all those Shirley MacLaine awards in your bathroom and I wondered why you think she's so special. I've been told that she's really a horrible person."

She looked me straight in the eye and said, "You son of a bitch!"

Whenever Danny came to Boston he stayed either at the Ritz or at our home. He was keenly interested in my family and me, and we loved him. When my daughter Kitty, living then in San Jose, California, was having marital problems, it was Danny who flew up from Los Angeles regularly to comfort her, later to call me with words of consolation.

Danny wanted to know everything about me. Once he insisted I show him the house where I was born. I drove him to 254 Western Avenue in Cambridge. He got out of the car and walked around the house. "Okay," he said. "Let's go." He had nothing more to say.

There was never any overt praise exchanged between Danny

Beating Time

and me. I met him once on his arrival at Logan Airport. "Danny," I said, "I've got something to show you." I drove him to Somerville, where the city had recently honored me. The Winter Hill Community School had named its two sections for two Somerville High graduates: Pie Traynor, the famous third baseman of the Pittsburgh Pirates, and myself. One section was the Pie Traynor Physical Education Center, the other the Harry Ellis Dickson Arts and Humanities Center. Danny looked thoughtfully at the bronze plaque with my name and likeness. "It looks like you're dead!" he said.

14

Guest Soloists and Koussevitzky

~ One of the great joys in being with the Boston Symphony Orchestra was meeting and playing with world-famous artists. Serge Koussevitzky's relationship with soloists was always ambiguous. He was not a good accompanist. His ego stood in the way of his being subservient to another's interpretation, and indeed soloists were few and far between during his tenure. On one occasion, there was a real musical catastrophe at a Friday afternoon concert. During the finale of the Prokofiev G Minor Violin Concerto with Jascha Heifetz, Koussey became confused and actually lost his place. He kept turning pages with his left hand while flailing the baton with his right, never catching up with the soloist. Heifetz finished a bar ahead of the orchestra, then refused, for a long while, to come out for a bow.

The appearance of Heifetz was always looked forward to with great excitement. "The world's greatest violinist," as he is still remembered even after his death, would appear at rehearsals impeccably dressed in suit and tie, his face devoid of expression. After being introduced by the conductor, Heifetz would nod at the orchestra with the same impassive face and then begin to play with

Beating Time

the utmost musicality and technical perfection. We never heard his voice, for when he stopped for corrections, he spoke very softly and only to the conductor. Once we did catch a few words when in the Beethoven Violin Concerto Koussevitzky expected a ritard that Heifetz did not make.

"But Jascha," Koussey said, "it is tradition!"

"Bad tradition," answered Heifetz, and there was no ritard.

In my second year with the orchestra, another soloist was the celebrated pianist Josef Hofmann, who, we soon surmised, had little respect for Koussevitzky. At the very first rehearsal of the Schumann Piano Concerto there was a feeling of hostility in the air. Hofmann kept stopping and giving directions to Koussevitzky, who was getting more and more embarrassed. It seemed to us in the orchestra that Hofmann was consciously trying to do just that—embarrass Koussevitzky. The performance was frightening. Hofmann seemed purposely to use excessive rubato in order to intimidate Koussevitzky. Hofmann never again played with the Boston Symphony.

Not every soloist with the BSO was as contentious as Hofmann. We always looked forward to the appearances of Artur Rubinstein, both in performance and recording. The conversations with him during intermissions were witty and wonderful. He spoke many languages, was the friend and confidant of kings and queens, and had an inexhaustible supply of charming anecdotes. About himself he said: "The young pianists of today play rings around me. But I still think I am a better musician." When Rubinstein was already in his late seventies, he came to record with us two piano concertos. The session in Symphony Hall began at 7:00 P.M., with Charles Munch conducting. Well past midnight, after both the Brahms D Minor and the Tchaikovsky First were recorded, Rubin-

Guest Soloists and Koussevitzky

stein asked if we could start over again. Both Munch and the musicians refused.

In the late 1950s, when relations between the Soviet Union and the United States began to ease, the celebrated Russian violinist David Oistrakh came to New York to give a recital at Carnegie Hall, to tremendous accolades. Shortly after this he was invited to play with the Boston Symphony, and I had the privilege of meeting him at his hotel and driving him to Symphony Hall for his first rehearsal. While Oistrakh was practicing backstage, word came from the office of James Petrillo, the head of the musician's union, that no permission had been given for a nonunion member to play with us. There was some delay as our management tried to negotiate on the telephone with union officials. Finally, permission was given and an international scandal was avoided. The incident was closed, and we enjoyed some wonderful concerts and recordings with Oistrakh.

Some time later another Russian violinist, Leonid Kogan, came to play with us, and again I was asked to escort him. Once, after a rehearsal, Kogan asked me if he could drive my car. It was a terrifying experience. He drove like a madman. I had visions of being stopped by a policeman and having to explain what this mad Russian was doing endangering the lives of American citizens. While he was driving Kogan asked me, "What kind of car is this?" When I told him that it was an Oldsmobile, he said, "I have better one in Moscow. I have Buick Special!"

One of my fondest memories is that of the great cellist Gregor Piatigorsky. He was a giant of a man, well over six feet tall, and looked somewhat like the Italian fighter Primo Carnera. There the resemblance stopped. Piatigorsky was a kind, warm, affectionate man, almost childlike in his openness and in his concern for others. He was also a great raconteur, and we spent many hours listening to his stories, some so fantastic that he probably had made them up.

Piatigorsky constantly complained about his fate as a musician. Whenever he came to Boston and I would ask: "Grischa, how are you?" his answer was always the same: "Lousy! Goddamn profession, always traveling, always worried, always nervous. Lousy profession!" One day in Symphony Hall, after a concert in which he had played magnificently, a group of us was sitting in the green room and the question of nervousness came up.

"Grischa," I said, "you don't appear at all nervous on stage."

"Yes," he said, "I am good actor. Before concert I am sitting in my room shivering like a baby. After all these years! Lately I even try psychology. I talk to myself: 'Grischa, you are the great Piatigorsky!'"

"Well," I asked, "does it help?"

"No," he replied, "I don't believe myself."

I was not quite old enough nor was I long enough in the orchestra to have played with the great violinist Fritz Kreisler, who had performed many times with the BSO under conductors prior to Koussevitzky. In the early years of Tanglewood, during the 1940s, Kreisler used to spend the summers in the Berkshires, and he frequently attended BSO concerts. Word came one day that he was ill with pneumonia at the hospital in Pittsfield. George Zazofsky and I were delegated to visit him. It was a memorable visit. Kreisler was old, feeble, and quite deaf, but his mind was alert. We had a wonderful conversation as he remembered his performances with the Boston Symphony. He told us of an incident one Friday afternoon in Symphony Hall when he almost played the wrong piece.

Guest Soloists and Koussevitzky

Pierre Monteux was conducting, and since both Kreisler and Monteux knew the standard violin concerto repertoire thoroughly, they decided a rehearsal was not necessary. Kreisler came onstage to play the Beethoven Concerto and, after tuning, held his violin by his side expecting that concerto's long introduction. The printed program, however, called for the Mendelssohn Concerto, which has only a bar-and-a-half introduction—about two seconds of music—before the violin enters. When Kreisler heard that short introduction, he almost decapitated himself as he quickly brought his violin to his chin. He played the entire concerto flawlessly, but during the applause he admonished Monteux: "Why didn't you say Mendelssohn?"

Another legendary musical figure who appeared before my time with the BSO was the great cellist Pablo Casals. I had the privilege of spending an afternoon with him at his home in Puerto Rico in the late 1960s.

Jane and I, on our way to the Virgin Islands, made a stopover in Puerto Rico. I had been in touch with a friend and colleague, the pianist Jesus Maria Sanroma, who lived there, and he had arranged the meeting. It was unforgettable. Casals, in his nineties, was alert and charmingly hospitable. He reminisced about his concerts with the Boston Symphony so many years back, and was eager to know about the orchestra. "Your conductor, Leinsdorf," he asked, "how do you like him? Let's go into the other room where you can tell me your real opinion—just between us."

Before we left he asked his young wife, Martita, to bring out a bottle of wine. "This is in your honor," he said. "It was a present from Ben-Gurion."

Perhaps the most energetic of all concert artists is the violinist Isaac Stern. Now in his seventies, he may have slowed down, but

Beating Time

if so, it is not evident. Until recently he played more concerts per year than any other artist, yet found time to engage in numerous humanitarian and civic pursuits. Extremely articulate as a writer, speaker, and raconteur, Stern was almost singlehandedly responsible for the preservation of Carnegie Hall, which, but for his efforts, would have become an office building or a parking lot. At rehearsals Stern was the most easygoing of all violinists. He genuinely enjoyed what he was doing and seemed to invite the orchestra to make music with him. His camaraderie with the musicians was quite in contrast to Heifetz's aloofness. Yet for some strange reason, musicians in the orchestra resented Stern's friendly approach. One of our clarinetists, Pat Cardillo, was highly insulted because Stern dared to make a direct musical suggestion to him instead of transmitting his wishes through the conductor. At rehearsals, Stern was apt to approach each section of the orchestra, making comments and suggestions while he was playing. As for myself, I rather liked that way of making music. It certainly was not intended on Stern's part to be anything but a means to a better performance.

In my lifetime there were performers of whom I was in awe. Great violinists—Jascha Heifetz, Isaac Stern, Itzhak Perlman. Great pianists—Vladimir Horowitz, Artur Rubinstein. Great cellists—Gregor Piatigorsky, Yo-Yo Ma, Mstislav Rostropovich, who also served with distinction as conductor of the National Symphony in Washington. Of course, there have been others, too, but these magnificent artists stand out in my memory.

Each performer is different. Heifetz was austere. Rostropovich, on the other hand, was very gregarious, a lovable man who kissed everybody. Horowitz was also extremely reserved. In his early years he could be irrational, and he canceled many concerts be-

Guest Soloists and Koussevitzky

cause of his nervousness. The story went that Horowitz's manager would advertise in *Musical America*, "Next year, Vladimir Horowitz will be available for a limited number of cancellations." This great pianist actually had to be pushed onto the stage. For about twelve years Horowitz gave up playing entirely.

Soloists are the "spice" added to an orchestral concert, and I admire them enormously, not only for their talent but also for their durability. Heifetz once ridiculed the notion that a sensitive musician must be fragile. "The delicate concert artist," he said, "must have the nerves of a bullfighter, the digestion of a peasant, the hide of a politician, and the tact of a nightclub hostess."

Playing the music of modern composers also added much to my life in the Boston Symphony Orchestra. I remember two of the greatest composers of the twentieth century—Igor Stravinsky and Béla Bartók. Stravinsky came to the Boston Symphony several times to conduct his own compositions. He was a severe man, completely lacking in humor. He always appeared onstage during rehearsals with a Turkish towel wrapped around his shoulders. He conducted with an angular motion, very awkward, and accompanied his own motions with grunts and snorts and always seemed to be in a world by himself. When one of the players asked him about a certain note in the ballet *Jeux de Cartes*, Stravinsky peered at the score and said, "I will study it and tell you later." He did display a kind of self-deprecating humor when I showed him an all-Stravinsky program I had conducted at a Young People's Concert. "Did they throw things at you?" he asked.

Béla Bartók never conducted our orchestra, but he sat in the balcony overlooking the stage when we first rehearsed the premiere of his Concerto for Orchestra, a composition commissioned by Koussevitzky. Bartók was a small, wizened, white-haired man, whose pale face contrasted with his fiery eyes. I remember his constantly standing up in the balcony shouting: "No, it is too slow!" "No, it is too fast!" "No, it is too loud . . . too soft!" Eventually Koussevitzky asked him to "take-it a pencil and pepper and make-it your observations" (Koussey always added his own personal suffix "it" to verbs)—at which point Bartók started to write and did so throughout the entire rehearsal. Such was Koussevitzky's great power of influence that after the break, when Bartók had left, Koussevitzky announced to the orchestra: "Gentlemen, I had a long talk with Bartók and he said everything was fine."

Paul Hindemith was very matter-of-fact, a utilitarian composer about whom it was said that composing to him was like writing a letter. Hindemith had no illusions about himself; he was a composer and that was his craft. I remember talking to him backstage at Carnegie Hall before we went out to play his *Mathis der Mahler* Symphony. I asked him, "Aren't you going to hear it?" "No," he said, "I know how it goes."

Aaron Copland was a particular favorite of Koussey's, and we often saw Copland sitting in the first balcony over the stage, listening to a rehearsal of one of his works. As he did with every composition, Koussevitzky took the piece over as one of his own and would play it "his" way. "Aaron, why do you write *mezzoforte*? *Mezzoforte* is the most baddest nuance qui existe!" And Copland would agree. He tried the same tactic with Hindemith and failed. Once, with Hindemith in the balcony, Koussey tried to discuss a musical point in *Mathis der Mahler*. "Whatever I wrote, I meant," Hindemith said, and there was no more discussion. After that we seldom played Hindemith.

Walter Piston was a dear man, quiet, unassuming, self-deprecating, with a dry sense of humor. Piston once told me that

Guest Soloists and Koussevitzky

he was cashing a check and the bank clerk asked, "What do you do?" Piston answered, "I'm a composer." "Oh," she said, looking at him quizzically. A fine composer who lived in Belmont, a suburb of Boston, and taught at Harvard, Piston became "court composer" for the Boston Symphony, and we premiered most of his new works.

Indeed, Serge Koussevitzky was responsible for introducing more new works by American composers than any other conductor. The list is long, although some are now almost forgotten. There were premieres by William Schuman, Roy Harris, Samuel Barber, Howard Hanson, David Diamond, Harold Shapero, Lukas Foss, Irving Fine, and Leonard Bernstein, to name a few.

Koussevitzky used to try to spread his enthusiasm for any new work to the members of the orchestra. More than once he would announce, "Dis is di greatest since Beethoven!" However, if after a few performances the piece had elicited a less than enthusiastic response from audiences, it would quietly disappear.

After encouraging the composer Irving Fine to become a conductor, Koussevitzky once attended a concert led by Fine. After the performance, Koussey rushed backstage. "Fine, Fine," he shouted. The composer, thrilled by Koussevitzky's praise, beamed. "Fine," Koussey continued, "that was awful!"

15

Arthur Fiedler and the Boston Pops

ᗌ It will probably come as a surprise to some to discover that Arthur Fiedler was not the first conductor of the Boston Pops. Although his name became synonymous with the Pops during his nearly fifty years as conductor, he was actually the Pops' eighteenth. "The Boston Symphony Promenade Concerts" began in 1885 in the original home of the Boston Symphony Orchestra—the Boston Music Hall, now the Orpheum Theater—and the first conductor was Adolf Neuendorff. In 1900, when the orchestra moved to its present home, Symphony Hall, the Promenade Concerts became "The Symphony Hall Pops," and after that merely "The Boston Pops." Fiedler began conducting the Pops in 1930, and he achieved a success and popularity never approached by any of the first seventeen conductors, all Europeans.

I first met Arthur Fiedler in December 1931, just before I left for Germany. I was introduced to him by Boaz Piller, a bassoonist in the Boston Symphony Orchestra. When Fiedler learned I was on my way to Germany, he asked me to take a five-pound can of coffee to his parents in Berlin. At the German border I had to pay a duty of three marks (about seventy-five cents), for which I was never reimbursed by Fiedler. Although I jokingly mentioned it to

Beating Time

him from time to time, he would always reach into his pocket and come up empty. I became reacquainted with Fiedler during my WPA days when I was conducting the WPA orchestra and he was a member of the advisory board of the Federal Music Project in Boston.

A few weeks before the start of the 1955 Pops season, Fiedler was told he needed an operation. He knew that he wouldn't be well enough to open the season, so he asked me to take over for the first few weeks. As it turned out, I conducted almost the entire season. The following season, at Arthur's suggestion, I was appointed assistant conductor. Until that time Fiedler had never considered having an assistant. He had conducted every night, six nights a week, for ten weeks.

Fiedler was the most insecure, suspicious man I ever knew, as well as the stingiest. He trusted nobody, not even his wife and family. In retrospect I believe he accepted me because he felt I was no threat. He had seen me conduct during the WPA days and had confidence that I could do the job. I had also done him a favor.

In 1959 Arthur had been contracted to conduct a Pops concert in Lowell, Massachusetts, an annual benefit for a local hospital. Some months prior to this Fiedler and the Pops had taken part in a movie about Norway, and now the king of Norway had invited Arthur to the opening of the film. Of course all expenses would be paid, and Arthur was eager to go. There was one hitch. The Lowell concert was on the same night as the Oslo opening. Fiedler asked the Lowell people to release him from his contract and suggested me in his place. They were no fools. They would accept me and release Fiedler under the condition that he pay my fee. Arthur called me into his room and with a long and sad face told me about his dilemma.

Arthur Fiedler and the Boston Pops

"Don't worry, Arthur," I said. "I'll do it for nothing."

"You will?" His eyes lit up.

I conducted the concert and actually lost money, since I was not paid even my usual fee for playing violin. Fiedler did eventually send me a check—after our personnel manager shamed him into it.

Although I was thrilled with my new job and still played in the BSO, I paid for the privilege. For years Leo Panasevich, a fellow violinist, kept reminding me, "Without us, you would be nobody." One morning after conducting a Pops concert the night before, I was back in my usual seat in the orchestra. Matt Ruggiero, our first bassoonist, asked me, "Where were you last night?"

In spite of everything, I admired Fiedler—though certainly not for his generosity or altruism. He was a good conductor who knew how to whip an orchestra into shape. He had good "ears"; he had an uncanny ability to detect wrong notes, and he knew how to balance an orchestra. The one thing he lacked was feeling. He seemed embarrassed when the music called for emotion. Fiedler was completely unhistrionic in his conducting and slavishly followed what was written in the score. The score was his Bible, and it irritated him when he heard something that was not on the printed page of the score. One morning, at rehearsal with the jazz trumpeter Dizzy Gillespie, Arthur realized that what Gillespie was playing was not in his score. He stopped the orchestra. "What are you doing?" he asked. Gillespie answered, "Maestro, never mind what I'm doing, you just keep it a-goin'!" Fiedler reluctantly went back to beating time. A few minutes later Gillespie muttered under his breath, "Man, he don't know where *one* is!"

Rehearsals with Fiedler were almost always adversarial. There seemed to be a constant war between him and the players. If he

Beating Time

made a correction or suggestion, it was accepted grudgingly; yet they had high respect for him as a musician.

He didn't always have his own way. We were once rehearsing a Beatles tune called "I Wanna Hold Your Hand," which Fiedler wickedly programed in spite of the expected disapproval of the proper Bostonians. The arrangement, by Richard Hayman, called for the violinists and violists to put their instruments down and clap their hands. Fiedler looked down at Eugene Lehner, a Hungarian and one of our distinguished violists, who sat with his arms folded. "Why aren't you clapping?" Fiedler asked. "I did not learn hand clapping at the Budapest Conservatory," Lehner retorted.

Fiedler's penuriousness was legendary. He never had a manager to whom he would have had to pay the usual 20 percent commission, and instead used a Boston Symphony secretary to handle his bookings. In his own household he paid all the expenses himself, and when he was on tour the bills (food, laundry, electric, gas) were sent directly to him. In later years, when he became ill and was in the hospital, he insisted that all bills be given to him personally. Next to his bed was his checkbook, and once, while Fiedler was asleep, his lawyer surreptitiously looked into it and was amazed to find a balance of nearly half a million dollars!

At the close of each Pops season Arthur used to give a party for the musicians, but always reluctantly. During the last week he would ask me, "Should I give another party? They don't like me. Why should I do it?" Each year I would convince him that they really liked him. So he would bring in all the records of previous parties on small pieces of paper and then begin the ritual of ordering the hot dogs, rolls, beer, and so on. Fiedler would call the wholesale provision company and the following conversation would inevitably take place:

Arthur Fiedler and the Boston Pops

"Hello, Sam, Fiedler here. It's time for that goddamn party again. Last year they ate up thirty pounds of hot dogs. Let's make it thirty-five. I'll be over to pick them up." Bill Shisler, our librarian, would drive him. The big incentive for his going personally was that he was always given a free salami. Once I said to him, "You know, Arthur, you should be ashamed of yourself, a man in your position."

"How would you do it?" he asked.

"Well," I said, "I would call a caterer and have him arrange everything."

"Maybe you can afford it," he protested. "You married a rich woman."

Arthur Fiedler was a loner. I believe I was as close to him as anyone was, and that wasn't very close. I think he liked me and tolerated my taking advantage of his "good nature." For years there was a kind of running battle between us over my practice of stealing batons from his drawer. Although he really didn't mind it—he had an abundant supply, which he got free—it became a point of contention that he exploited to the limit.

After his last Pops concert he went back to the green room and collapsed. Cleve Morrison, our stage manager, came back to the tuning room looking for me. "The boss is asking for you," he said. That seemed strange to me because Fiedler was not one to ask for anyone no matter what his predicament. I hurried back to the green room, where paramedics were working on him before taking him to the hospital. His eyes were closed and I wasn't sure he was conscious.

"Did you want to see me, Arthur?" I asked.

Fiedler opened his eyes, and with a satanic grin he asked, "Did you swipe my baton?"

Beating Time

"No, Arthur," I answered, "it's right here on the table."

"Okay," he said, and closed his eyes.

To the world Arthur Fiedler presented an image that was warm and friendly. The public perception of him was that of a kindly Santa Claus who loved everybody. Actually, he had a tremendous commitment to his audiences, even a kind of love for them (in bulk), but a cynical contempt for each of them individually. Fiedler never spoke to his audience. If there was a special announcement to be made, it was left to me to make it. In all the years I knew him, I never saw a sign of warmth or affection toward anyone except his dog. Once, in a TV interview, the host facetiously asked Fiedler, "Is it true you don't like children or dogs?" The answer was, "I like dogs!"

I never saw Arthur kiss his own children, and even when they came to Symphony Hall, the greetings with their father in the green room seemed formal and standoffish. For some reason Fiedler hated to be called Daddy, so the children addressed him as Papa. Arthur Fiedler was an innate male chauvinist, and completely honest about it. He used to say that every girl should be conscripted into nursing for at least a year. He abhorred women in the orchestra. Once, at a concert celebrating the tenth anniversary of Quincy Market at Faneuil Hall, Fiedler was conducting a Pops Esplanade Orchestra made up largely of substitutes. One of the guests was Joan Mondale, the wife of Walter Mondale, who was then vice president. After the concert there was a late supper at the home of Governor Michael Dukakis attended by Fiedler, Mrs. Mondale, and a few others. During the conversation, Mrs. Mondale said to Fiedler, "I was interested to see so many women in the orchestra," to which he replied, "Looked like a cooking school,

Arthur Fiedler and the Boston Pops

didn't it!" Mrs. Mondale wrote me afterward saying that she hadn't realized there were still people like Arthur Fiedler.

When Fiedler died in 1979, I had a flicker of hope that I might be chosen to succeed him, a hope soon discarded because I knew in my heart that the management would be looking for a younger man, and I was then already in my seventies. Happily, they chose John Williams, the eminently talented Hollywood composer. It was André Previn, the composer, pianist, and conductor, who recommended Williams and persuaded his friend and colleague to take the job.

Although John Williams had always conducted his own film music with various orchestras, he had never before been the established conductor of a concert orchestra. Williams reluctantly agreed to take on the Boston Pops. Following fifty years of Fiedler was no easy task. He turned out to be the perfect choice; a man with a serious classical background and training—a graduate of the Juilliard School in New York—but with knowledge of and feeling for American popular music. John Williams has been spectacularly successful, elevating the Pops to new heights of popularity. This was evidenced by the increased audiences in Boston and throughout the world through the media of radio, television, recordings, and periodic tours in this country and Japan.

Before John Williams came to Boston I had expected him to be a flamboyant, self-centered "Hollywood" type. But I found just the opposite. He is a sincere, quiet, modest, articulate, and intelligent human being. Perhaps I can add the word *sensitive*, for it was his sensitivity that caused a break with the orchestra after he had been in Boston a couple of years.

During a rehearsal of a new arrangement there was some hissing

Beating Time

of disapproval among the players, a childish practice of musicians whenever a new piece is rehearsed for the first time. John left the stage in anger and, when he came back a few minutes later, announced that he would not return the following year. I tried to explain to him that nothing personal was intended, that this behavior went on all during Fiedler's tenure, but John was intransigent. It was an insult not only to him but also to the arranger, he maintained. I told him that Fiedler was never bothered by the expressions or opinions of the players. In his tough, insensitive way he would say to the orchestra: "I don't care if you don't like it. You're paid to play, so just play it!"

It took a year's contemplation and numerous apologies for John to reconsider, but he did return. The musicians kept their opinions to themselves, and a mutual respect existed between conductor and players. In 1993, after his fourteenth year with the Pops, John Williams again announced he was leaving, this time a friendly departure.

John Williams's association with the Pops produced a major accomplishment. He brought a sense of seriousness, call it dignity, to the Pops. Certainly under Fiedler the Pops was well attended and financially successful. But there was always the feeling that it was the second cousin to the Boston Symphony. It was the tolerated distant relative that brought in the money.

Indeed, when Fiedler first became the conductor of the Pops in 1930, his relationship with Serge Koussevitzky was not a happy one. Koussey despised the Pops and everything it stood for. His recurrent remark at the first rehearsal at Tanglewood, after the ten-week Pops season, was: "Vot happened to my orchestra? Too much Popst!"

The only time Arthur Fiedler conducted the BSO was in January

Arthur Fiedler and the Boston Pops

1932 when both Koussevitzky and Burgin were ill. The one other time Fiedler was scheduled to conduct a pair of regular Boston Symphony concerts, the offer was withdrawn. Koussey had read a poster in front of Symphony Hall advertising a concert by Frank Sinatra with an orchestra conducted by Arthur Fiedler. This so infuriated him that he canceled Fiedler's BSO concerts.

My own association with the Pops continues, and as of this writing I am the "elder statesman" called upon, in addition to conducting some regular seasonal concerts, to do the numerous "outside" concerts. One of these is the annual "Pops by the Sea" concert on Cape Cod, outdoors in the square facing the Hyannis Town Hall. A benefit for the local arts council, it has attracted more than fifteen thousand listeners per concert over the past ten years.

Each year a local celebrity has been invited to "conduct" a march. The results have been interesting but uneven. Perhaps the most authoritative was Walter Cronkite, who, I learned, used to play in a band. The others were also luminaries in myriad fields: Art Buchwald, who attends each year and invariably comes backstage to ask, "I was the best, wasn't I?"; Mike Wallace, a former violin pupil of mine; Beverly Sills; Julia Child, who conducted with a soup spoon; and Regis Philbin, who didn't quite stop with the orchestra. "I hate it," he said, "when they don't finish with me." An intermission visitor, Arnold Schwarzenegger, came backstage. "Let me feel your muscles," he demanded. We then waxed into German (he was born in Graz, Austria), to the chagrin of Philbin, who kept interrupting. "You're talking about me, aren't you?" he grumbled.

"It's fun to be a Pops conductor," Fiedler used to say. "You never know who you're going to meet."

Beating Time

During the intermission of a Pops concert in Symphony Hall one of our trustees, Michael Kelleher, brought Walt Dropo, the first baseman of the Boston Red Sox, in to see Fiedler. I was in the room and was also introduced, when in walked George Moleux, the first bass of the Pops. I sensed some humor in the situation, and introduced Moleux to Dropo. "George, meet Walt Dropo. He also plays first base."

Moleux, who knew absolutely nothing about baseball, asked Dropo, "What orchestra?"

"I play for the Red Sox," replied Dropo.

"How many basses do you have?" Moleux asked Dropo.

"We have three," responded Dropo.

"Oh, must be a small orchestra." And Moleux left the room.

16

Youth Concerts: A Dream Realized

⌐ Unlike most symphony orchestras in the United States, which devote a large part of their schedule to playing for young people, the Boston Symphony had, over the years, done little in this field. There were occasional special concerts for children. I remember attending one as a high school student with Serge Koussevitzky conducting and Wallace Goodrich, the dean of the New England Conservatory of Music, commenting.

For some years the late Ernest Schelling presented a series of youth concerts in Jordan Hall, an auditorium about half the size of Symphony Hall, with an orchestra of Boston Symphony players. Later Wheeler Beckett presented an annual series of concerts in Symphony Hall. These concerts were quite successful, yet for some reason they came to an end, and for about a dozen years there were no young people's concerts in Boston.

My wife once asked me, "Why doesn't the Boston Symphony Orchestra give concerts for young people?" I decided to find out. When I presented the idea to Tod Perry, the orchestra's manager, he was not encouraging. "We don't think a Cadillac orchestra should engage in Ford activities," he said. Tod offered to cooperate, however, if I undertook the task of organizing the concerts.

137

Beating Time

He would allow me the use of the hall and the music library, but the musicians would have to be engaged individually and we could not use the name of the Boston Symphony Orchestra.

Jane, undaunted, went ahead with plans. She assembled a small committee of women and a trio of "angels": affable, affluent, civic-minded businessmen who agreed to underwrite the concerts. To these three—Irving Rabb, Leo Pistorino, and Max Wasserman—the children of Massachusetts owe a debt of gratitude.

"Youth Concerts at Symphony Hall" was launched. Typically, Jane stayed in the background and insisted that the dynamic Felicia Kutten take over as chairwoman. She also enlisted the talents of Anita Kurland, a bright, arts-oriented, dedicated lady. Anita used her considerable skills to organize and encourage more than a hundred communities throughout Massachusetts to participate. (Anita, a dear friend for many years, is now my agent, arranging concert engagements for me throughout the world.)

There was at that time a state supervisor of music who did not take kindly to having youngsters come to Symphony Hall to hear Beethoven. "They'll throw things," she said. We convinced her to go along with us, however, and after the first concert, in 1959, she became an enthusiastic supporter. We did indeed play Beethoven and the children were attentive.

Isaac Stern, who was appearing with the Boston Symphony that week, agreed to be the soloist at our first concert, on Saturday morning. I remember how quietly interested the youngsters were, not only in his playing, but in his down-to-earth remarks and explanations. He asked how many played the violin and, after getting a show of hands, said, "It's tough to play the violin, isn't it? You probably get discouraged as I did. But you must stick with it." He went on to explain how musicians must train their hearing,

Youth Concerts: A Dream Realized

their muscular coordination, and so on. Stern played a G-major scale, slightly out of tune, and with a rather unpleasant, steely sound. "That is the way we all sound when we begin," he said. "But with practice you develop your ear and control, and you begin to sound better." He played the scale again, this time beautifully, and the audience burst into applause. We then played the finale of the Mendelssohn Concerto, first illustrating the themes, showing how the composer sometimes allows the orchestra to play the melody while the soloist accompanies it and vice versa, then the entire movement without pause. This humanistic approach to music, so charmingly carried out by Stern, is what we have been striving for in our youth concerts ever since.

"Youth Concerts at Symphony Hall" have now become "The Boston Symphony Youth Concerts" and are part of the orchestra's regular schedule. The orchestra plays fifteen of these concerts a year and has already welcomed more than a million youngsters. One of the important activities is the annual competition for high school soloists; the winners appear with the orchestra. Over the years, many musical careers have been encouraged. Four present members of the Boston Symphony Orchestra are former winners of the Youth Concert Competitions: Lawrence Wolfe, bass; Ronald Lefkowitz and Victor Romanul, violins; and Sato Knudsen, cello.

The BSO Youth Concerts have been beneficial, not only for those talented youngsters who have been encouraged to continue as performers, but also for those who have been introduced to the magic of music through the Boston Symphony and thus started on their way to becoming talented listeners. I often encounter people who tell me they heard their first concerts under my direction at the Youth Concerts and are now symphony subscribers;

Beating Time

some of them are serving on symphony boards in their own communities.

Over the years we have received thousands of letters from young listeners: "I didn't want to go, but my teacher made me," wrote one fourth-grade boy. "But I liked it." Another youngster, a girl, wrote: "I felt like crying in 'Clair de Lune' but I was too ashamed." In a batch of letters, evidently an assignment from the teacher, one boy wrote: "Dear Mr. Dickson. It was a wonderful concert. I couldn't go because I was sick but my sister told me." One boy of eleven wrote, "Dear Mr. Dickson: I enjoyed the concert very much. I have an ear for music and it listened to every bit." A girl wrote: "I asked my mother why they don't serve popcorn and soda at the concerts, and she said in Symphony Hall they serve only caviar and champagne!"

Organizing a symphony concert for youngsters is a formidable task that involves an enormous amount of detail and planning. Were it not for our dedicated chairpersons in some one hundred communities throughout Massachusetts, who handle the myriad details, such as tickets and transportation, these concerts could never survive. Even the policemen who direct the traffic on concert mornings cooperate. At a concert for handicapped children, an anonymous police captain supplied lollipops for more than two thousand youngsters.

Occasionally there arises the problem of a lost or strayed youngster. Long after a concert had ended on one wintry Saturday morning a little girl was found wandering outside the hall. A policeman brought her into the green room, where some of the committee ladies and I were still discussing the concert. She told us her bus had left without her. "What happened?" I asked. "Oh," she answered, "I was walking to the bus with my school chums, but I stopped to talk to a dog." A telephone call was made to her home, which was quite a distance from Boston, and her father grudgingly came to get her.

Our programs are varied, and we have played music from the pre-Baroque period to the ultramodern, including an occasional avant-garde piece, which is much easier for a young person, without adult prejudices, to accept than it is for his or her parents. We have even presented programs of jazz and music based on jazz, never attempting to influence the listeners, but presenting all the aspects of music and letting them make up their own minds.

Especially interesting to me was our experiment with music other than the loud and bombastic. Each program contained at least one short, quiet piece when the audience was invited to listen in silent contemplation. One of the more successful compositions was a work by the American composer Michael Colgrass, *As Quiet As . . .* Before playing it we announced that we were about to test the fine acoustics of Symphony Hall, and in the ensuing stillness dropped a pin on the stage, inviting those in the second balcony to listen for it. "Yes!" they cried.

If we have learned anything about young people, it is that we must never play down to them. I am firmly convinced that children's interests are not limited to special music for the young. They can listen to all kinds, including some too "deep" for their elders. The only compromise one need make is to their attention span. In this regard I used to follow the advice of a psychologist who once told me that a child's listening span could be measured by his or her age. An eight-year-old could listen to an eight-minute piece, a ten-year-old to a ten-minute piece, and so on.

Beating Time

Experience, however, has shown that unless there is a narration or visual activity, as in ballet or opera, the psychologist's advice should be somewhat modified.

Occasionally, when trying to protect their sensibilities, I have been sharply rebuked. One Saturday morning we played Strauss's *Till Eulenspiegel*, which I first explained with musical illustrations. When it came to the story of Till skipping merrily up the gallows (depicted by the saucy E-flat clarinet), I thought I would spare them and said, "And here Till skips up the steps of the gallows and disappears into thin air. And for all we know he is still skipping around somewhere." A week later I got a letter from an irate nine-year-old boy. "That's wrong," he wrote. "He was hung!"

Our final concert for some years had been a "youth participation" program in which we had invited both the Greater Boston Youth Symphony Orchestra and the New England Conservatory Youth Orchestra to join us in a final selection. Each student musician sat next to a Boston Symphony player, who took the inside seat. At one series of concerts we played the finale of Beethoven's Ninth Symphony with the choruses of four high schools, and in the final chorale the entire audience joined in singing (in English) the "Ode to Joy."

We have also presented original compositions by high school students. These students came from the neighboring city of Newton, where their teacher, the late Henry Lasker, a thoroughly trained professional composer and pianist, had demonstrated that young people can be taught to compose as well as to play. Their compositions were understandably derivative and imitative, but some showed surprising originality. The mere fact that high school students learn to compose and orchestrate their own works is remarkable; and to have their music played by a professional orchestra at a public concert gives these young people great incentive. Some of these fledgling composers have gone on to college to major in composition.

From time to time we have presented at our youth concerts father-and-son combinations in which a Boston Symphony musician has played with his son. A number of years ago Sherman Walt and his son Stephen played the Vivaldi Concerto for Two Bassoons, George Zazofsky and his son Peter played the Bach Double Violin Concerto, and Roger Voisin and his son Peter played the Vivaldi Concerto for Two Trumpets. I have followed with interest the careers of the young men involved. Peter Zazofsky was graduated from the Curtis Institute of Music in Philadelphia and went on to become an internationally famous soloist. Peter Voisin, now married, plays in the Syracuse Symphony Orchestra. As for Stephen Walt, he temporarily abandoned music in favor of an academic career, but has returned to his first love, the bassoon, and enjoys a double career. Now that more and more women have joined the BSO, our hope is one day to present a mother and daughter, mother and son, or father and daughter.

From time to time I have introduced famous conductors to our young audiences. Charles Munch, Erich Leinsdorf, Arthur Fiedler, and Seiji Ozawa have all conducted segments of our programs. William Steinberg and Sir John Barbirolli have attended our concerts and were presented to the youngsters. An entire delegation of Russian composers, headed by Dmitri Shostakovich and Dmitri Kabalevsky, made their appearance one Saturday morning, and after we played a piece by Shostakovich, I had the pleasure of introducing him from the stage.

During our more than thirty years of existence we have tried to bring a sense of participation to these concerts. At one series we

Beating Time

played Prokofiev's *Peter and the Wolf* while exhibiting slides that the Boston-area primary school students had conceived and executed. At other series of concerts we have had student narrators, student dancers, and student singers. And we have had compositions written expressly for us. One of the most successful has been Michael Colgrass's *The Earth's a Baked Apple,* in memory of Martin Luther King, Jr., written for a youth chorus and orchestra.

Whether or not these concerts add to young people's "culture" (a word I abhor), they do serve to introduce a certain amount of beauty into their lives.

17

On the Road:
The BSO Away from Boston

⌁ Perhaps few people have ever thought about the problems of logistics connected with a tour by a major symphony orchestra. Moving more than a hundred musicians, management, support staff, and well over ten tons of instruments and baggage from one city to another and one country to another requires careful planning. The Boston Symphony Orchestra packs wardrobe trunks, trunks full of music, music stands, a conductor's podium, nine big bass trunks, eleven cello trunks, two harps, five or six kettledrums, bass drums, snare drums, cymbals, xylophones, assorted other percussion instruments, all kinds of brass and woodwind instruments, and specially lined cases for the more-delicate stringed instruments.

Before each trip the BSO librarian makes sure that we've packed not only the music for all the scheduled programs but also extra music for emergencies. Once in Japan, when almost half the orchestra became ill, Charles Munch had to change the program and conduct a chamber orchestra.

The Beethoven *Eroica* Symphony is always carried on tours of

145

Beating Time

the orchestra. When President Roosevelt died in April 1945, word was received on the train to Philadelphia. That night we played a memorial concert for the late president, including the Funeral March from the *Eroica*. (That was not the first time our schedule had been influenced by President Roosevelt. Our concert at the Kleinhaus Auditorium in Buffalo, on December 7, 1941, had been interrupted for President Roosevelt's radio speech about the Japanese attack on Pearl Harbor. At the end of the concert, a very sober audience applauded perfunctorily and left the hall quietly.)

Beethoven's Third Symphony has become a kind of symbol of sadness in the orchestra. The day President Kennedy was assassinated, we learned just before our Friday afternoon concert that he had been shot. We did not know how seriously he was hurt until, after the first piece on the program, our two librarians suddenly appeared onstage to distribute the music for the *Eroica*.

When the orchestra began to travel by air, there arose a new problem—that of plane mishap. The full complement of the orchestra never flew on the same plane. The strings, woodwinds, brass, and percussion were evenly divided into two sections so that if something happened to one plane, the rest could still give a concert. Increased air safety has made this no longer necessary.

Out-of-town trips used to be much more exciting than they are today. Somehow or other, when we left Boston in our own Pullman train and, in some cases, lived on that train for two weeks, it was more glamorous than today's quick plane hops. Gone are those days when our wives would see us off at South Station in Boston and wave to us as our special train pulled out with banners flying, a big BSO ON TOUR sign at the rear of the train. Within minutes the poker game would start in the club car, a friendly game

On the Road: The BSO Away from Boston

that would end the next morning in Buffalo with a few winners and a few minus their week's salary.

A wonderful spirit of camaraderie existed on the trains. On my very first train trip I happened, as the result of drawing lots, to have a lower berth. When I offered it to my older colleague Leon Gorodetzky, he said: "No, I'd like to be fair about it. Let's toss a coin." I told him it wasn't necessary; he could have it anyway. But he insisted, we tossed, and I won.

"Look," I said, "I won, but you can still have it."

Not satisfied, he said, "No, let's toss again." I left him standing in the aisle as I crawled into the upper berth.

Those were the days when I discovered what an enormously large family I had. In almost every city a different relative showed up, sometimes with unpredictable results. We arrived in Cleveland one wintry afternoon, and on the station platform I saw a man walking up and down with a photograph in his hand, shouting "Dickson? Dickson?" I stopped him, introduced myself, and he said, "Come with me." Then it dawned on me: this was the husband of my mother's cousin, a cousin my mother had not seen since their early days in Russia some thirty years before. My mother had sent her a photograph of me.

I went home with my newly found relative to a tempestuous welcome. My mother's cousin was an obese, good-natured Jewish mother who, upon seeing me, burst into tears. "Just like your mother you look! I would know you anywhere!" she sobbed. "Come, I will make you something to eat." When I protested that I wasn't hungry, she said, "At least a glass of tea you'll have!" I had the tea. Then came a jolting pronouncement. "You will stay at least a couple of weeks." No, I told her, that was impossible. We

Beating Time

were playing in Cleveland that night and were leaving for Pittsburgh in the morning. "I won't let you go," she said. "You come here once in a lifetime and you think I will let you go in one day?"

"But I can't," I protested. "I'm here with the Boston Symphony Orchestra, not on a pleasure trip."

"How many are there in the orchestra?" she asked.

"A hundred and four," I answered.

"So," she said, "they certainly don't need you!"

"They may not need me," I said, "but I need them." It took a bit of arguing, but the next morning she released me. Not, however, before providing a lunch to "take with." It didn't matter that the train ride from Cleveland took only a couple of hours. I had to take the lunch. I can vividly remember distributing among my hungrier colleagues chunks of roast chicken and gefilte fish.

The first concert of every trip is the most trying—the night we discover what we forgot to bring. One night our tuba player opened his trunk only to find he had forgotten to pack his instrument. Some frantic telephone calls produced a tuba, a greatly appreciated loan from the local symphony player. On the first night as we dressed in front of our enormous wardrobe trunks, each one housing the needs of four people, there was a constant exchange—a pair of black socks for a white tie, a pair of trousers for a white vest, cuff links for a collar button.

On one of my early tours with the orchestra, I discovered I had left my white bow ties at home. A colleague loaned me one of his, the kind you have to tie yourself, which I couldn't do. When I asked him if he could tie it for me, he said, "Sure. But you'll have to lie down on the floor."

"Why?" I asked.

On the Road: The BSO Away from Boston

"Well," he said, "I used to help my father, who's an undertaker, and this is the only way I know how."

"No thanks," I said, and that night I learned how to tie a bow tie.

A number of years ago, when the orchestra traveled by Pullman, we played a concert at Constitution Hall in Washington and then left for New York and more concerts. George Zazofsky had recently acquired a beautiful Guadagnini violin, which he would not entrust to the regular orchestra instrument trunks, so he carried it with him. On this particular night he had unwisely left the violin in his upper berth while he went to the club car before the train started. After we left the station, George went back to his berth only to discover his violin was gone. Someone had come aboard while the train was in the station, as we later found out, and stolen it. Zazofsky was heartbroken; a violin to a musician is his best friend. About two weeks later the violin was discovered in a pawnshop in Alexandria, Virginia. The pawnbroker had given the thief five dollars—not for the violin, but for the new case.

Zazofsky was notified that he would have to come to the police station in Alexandria to redeem his violin. He immediately left for Alexandria and arrived at the police station fearing that the instrument had been damaged. The police captain handed him the violin case; Zazofsky quickly opened it and found, to his great relief, his precious violin unharmed. George thanked the policeman and was about to leave when the captain said, "Hold on! How do I know you're really a fiddler?" Zazofsky played "Danny Boy" for the captain and a group of officers in that police station in Alexandria, the most enthusiastic and appreciative audience he had ever had.

Since 1887 the BSO has been giving regular subscription con-

Beating Time

certs in New York. One week out of each month, from November to March, the orchestra goes on tour, playing in New York City and surrounding cities and towns.

Many of us used to eat regularly in a small restaurant on Seventh Avenue, the Carnegie Delicatessen. Over the years the restaurant became rather posh, with constantly improving decor. The proprietor, however, remained simple, kindly, and friendly. He greeted each of us every time we arrived with a "Hello, Boston! Welcome to New York!" Although he was acquainted with the entire orchestra, he knew not one name nor what instrument each played, and he had never been to a concert.

On one of our New York trips we were told he had suffered a heart attack and was in the hospital. The following season he was back, greeting us more profusely than ever. "I must tell you how much pleasure you gave me in the hospital," he said to us when we came in. "I used to watch your television broadcasts, and it was like meeting all my old friends. I recognized all of you. There was the lean corned beef; there was the double pastrami; there was the matzo ball soup. I knew you like brothers!"

Playing in different halls on our tours has made each of us sensitive to acoustics, and every member of the orchestra fancies himself an expert. Whenever we play in a new hall there are inevitable discussions and comparisons. A new hall to a musician is like a new suit. No matter how good it may look to others, if it doesn't feel right, it isn't right. A stage must be comfortable for the players; they must be able to hear their colleagues clearly and without distortion. If a hall feels good to a musician, it should sound good to the audience. Musicians have favorites, and usually they are the old friends: Carnegie Hall in New York, the Academy of Music in Philadelphia, Orchestra Hall in Chicago. Our own Symphony

On the Road: The BSO Away from Boston

Hall remains the most comfortable. Other orchestras also praise its qualities. Sound engineers have proclaimed it ideal for recording. I remember Stravinsky's enthusiasm when, after conducting a concert, he said, "This is surely the finest concert hall in the world."

Each hall has its own peculiar qualities. One is live, another dead. One is mellow, the other brittle and harsh. There seem to be many reasons for this variation of standards. Architects understandably want to express themselves with new ideas, new concepts of building structures, and, in some cases, radical designs. They don't always see eye to eye with the acoustical engineers, who have definite standards of sound measurement, reverberation, quality, and so on. The catastrophic acoustics of Philharmonic Hall at Lincoln Center—now Avery Fisher Hall—when it was first opened were the result, we are told, of unwillingness on the part of the architects to follow the exact specifications of acoustical experts, specifications of design and material. When we played there during opening week, it was a disaster. We could not hear each other, the balance was bad, and there was a feeling of playing in a large, open field. Such was the protest from critics and the public that the entire stage had to be torn up, the seats in the auditorium had to be redesigned, and changes had to be made in the walls and ceilings before the hall became suitable for concert performances.

New halls are also like new instruments. They must be "played in," and many good concert halls have become even better as they have grown older. Also, an orchestra learns to adjust itself to each hall. Occasionally, when we are to play in a brand-new hall and there is time, the conductor will call an "acoustical rehearsal" before the performance. When we played in the new Powell Symphony Hall in St. Louis, there was unfortunately no time for such a rehearsal, and we were completely unprepared for the overpowering blast of sound that was created when we played the opening of Wagner's *Meistersinger* Prelude. As the program progressed, however, the orchestra unconsciously tempered its dynamic range to suit the hall, and by the end of the concert we were "giving less but enjoying it more." This concert hall in St. Louis, beautifully remodeled from an old movie theater, has, after some minor acoustical adjustments and "playing-in," become one of the finest in the United States.

Occasionally an auditorium does not live up to its expectations. We had always heard that the Concertgebouw in Amsterdam was one of the finest halls in Europe, yet for some reason we found it one of the most uncomfortable to play in. On the other hand, the Grosser Musikvereinsaal in Vienna was a joy; it reminded us very much of our own Symphony Hall in Boston.

A good concert hall must have the quality of enveloping the listeners yet not overpowering them. Unlike a theater, where the proscenium separates the actors from the audience, a concert hall must be constructed so that the music washes over the listener. He or she must become part of the performance. The new Philharmonic Hall in Berlin is an example of a marvelous hall in which the audience surrounds the orchestra. We enjoy playing in that hall.

Playing in the Boston Symphony Orchestra becomes, after a while, a way of life. The rigorous schedule of daily rehearsals and concerts, the seasonal changes from winter schedule to the spring Pops concerts, then to the outdoor Esplanade concerts, and finally to our summer Berkshire Festival season, make our lives almost completely dependent on the orchestra. Romances bloom within

On the Road: The BSO Away from Boston

the family. A former first cellist married a colleague; our assistant first violist married Arthur Fiedler's secretary; the first violist married Koussevitzky's niece; and fate had a hand in the marriage of our clarinetist Patsy Cardillo.

We were on a midwinter orchestra tour, and after the Saturday night concert at Notre Dame University in South Bend, Indiana, we were in the small railroad station waiting for our train to take us to Chicago. It was a stormy, snowy, miserable night, and the train was very late. The orchestra took over the station. A few card games began on makeshift tables while in other areas of the station the usual clowning around and horseplay took place. Manny Valerio, the smallest man in the orchestra, paraded around in the enormous coat of Ludwig Juht, one of the largest members. Because the storm made uncertain the train's arrival time, everyone stayed inside, and the reverberating noise in the station became almost unbearable. The few local passengers seemed to be intimidated by this band of lunatics.

An attractive young lady, sitting in a corner trying to read, was constantly distracted by the shenanigans. Boaz Piller, one of the bassoonists, saw her, sat down next to her, and in his inimitable, charming, foreign-accented manner, tried to console her. "Don't be 'fraid," Boaz said. "Ve are all nice pipple." He then left her to seek out Pat Cardillo, one of the few unmarried men of the orchestra. Pat was playing cards, but Piller tore him away from the game to meet the young lady. There was an introduction in which the name Cardillo was mentioned but the girl's name was not. In fact, she refused to give it. After a few minutes of one-sided conversation, the train finally arrived at about 2:20 A.M. The girl hurried into the public passenger cars while Pat joined the orchestra in

Beating Time

the Boston Symphony cars. After the train had started and the inevitable poker game began, Patsy began to think about the beautiful, charming, frightened girl he had just met.

"What's her name?" asked Jimmy Stagliano, our first horn player. "I don't know," answered Cardillo, "she wouldn't give it to me. I could get it if I wanted it." And he went back through the train looking for the young lady. About an hour later, after the train had stopped at La Porte, Indiana, where she got off, Patsy came back to the orchestra car waving a piece of paper on which was written not only the girl's name but also her address and telephone number. The young lady from La Porte had spent the day shopping in South Bend and had missed the earlier train.

After a whirlwind courtship, at first by mail, then by telephone, then by journeys to La Porte, they were married. Mr. and Mrs. Pasquale Cardillo now have four delightful children, three boys and a girl, and a number of grandchildren of mixed Italian-Swedish, Midwestern–New England ancestry. All because of a missed train, a snowstorm, and a few other imponderables provided by fate and the tours of the Boston Symphony Orchestra.

18

Touring the Continent

⌐ Serge Koussevitzky had long held the dream of taking the Boston Symphony Orchestra to Europe, but it was not to be. Not until 1952, in Charles Munch's second year, did the orchestra tour Europe for the first time, with Munch and Pierre Monteux conducting. The tour began with a concert at the Théâtre National de l'Opéra in Paris on May 6 and another on May 8 at the Théâtre des Champs Elysées; then off to The Hague, Amsterdam, Brussels, and two performances in Frankfurt, followed by one in Berlin. Then Strasbourg, Lyon, back to Paris on the twenty-first, two concerts in Bordeaux, and our last concert of the tour: London, England, on May 26. The twenty-day, fifteen-concert tour was sponsored by the Congress for Cultural Freedom, which had chosen the Boston Symphony Orchestra to represent the United States.

The European critics were uniformly enthusiastic. The *Paris Presse-l'Intransigeant* reported: "One feels oneself in the presence of a great machine, beautifully equipped, and when this entire mechanism enters into action one is overwhelmed by its power, its subtlety, and its precision." The *Frankfurt Abendpost* said: "It seemed scarcely possible to evaluate the execution of this body with the usual adjective of critical judgment." From *Les Dernières Nouvelles*

Beating Time

d'Alsace (Strasbourg): "What a resplendent orchestra! To describe it at this moment of enthusiasm you would have to use several exclamations at once. You would say, 'Such strings, such woodwinds, such brass, such unity, such ensemble!'" The *Nouvelle République* (Bordeaux) commented: "The Festival of Bordeaux is decidedly ending in an apotheosis. . . . it has awaited till now its crowning. The philharmonic orchestra of Boston has brought this to pass."

Even the American critics accompanying the tour—Cyrus Durgin of the *Boston Globe*, R. F. Elie of the *Boston Herald*, Jay C. Rosenfeld of the *Berkshire Eagle*, and John Roderick of the *San Francisco Call-Bulletin*—were enthusiastic. "So far it has been one triumph after another for the touring Boston Symphony Orchestra," wrote Durgin. "The night they played in The Hague, they got a terrific ovation, although the people there are said to sit on their hands." Jay Rosenfeld wrote of the BSO's appearance in Holland: "Queen Juliana was quite bewildered by the reception her subjects gave the Boston Symphony Orchestra at The Hague. She didn't seem to know whether etiquette provided that a reigning monarch should continue to stand while such cheering went on or not. In any case, she joined in genuinely as the Boston Symphony Orchestra under Munch made its first stop on its European tour after the tremendously successful Paris debut."

The *Herald*'s critic, Elie, wrote on May 21: "The Boston Symphony Orchestra under conductor Charles Munch made a triumphant return to Paris tonight before a cheering crowd at the Théâtre National de l'Opéra. . . . The orchestra's tour . . . first time it has crossed the Atlantic since it was founded 71 years ago . . . has been an enormous success."

The concert at the Théâtre des Champs Elysées in Paris on May

Touring the Continent

8 was a memorable one. Munch had thoughtfully and most generously given this concert to Pierre Monteux, then age seventy-
seven, to conduct. Monteux's program ended with Stravinsky's *Rite
of Spring*, which Monteux had conducted at its premiere in the
same hall in 1913. What happened that night long ago is legend.
The audience hissed, there were catcalls, and at the end a fistfight.
Diaghilev, the director of the great Ballets Russes, was reduced to
tears; Stravinsky fled the hall in terror. On this night in 1952, with
Stravinsky again in the audience, there was complete decorum and
a sense of great excitement. At the close of the piece there was an
outburst of applause and bravos, as Stravinsky came running up
the aisle to the stage to embrace Monteux. "Enfin après quarante
ans!" he shouted. "At last, after forty years!"

In 1956 the Boston Symphony made its second European trip,
again with Charles Munch. The long tour began on August 24,
with a concert at the Theatre Royal in Cork, Ireland. We arrived
in Cork at the beginning of the tour two days before the concert
and were able to see a bit of the beautiful Irish countryside. Some
of us took an all-day bus trip, visiting the quaint towns and villages
that dot the southern part of Ireland—Limerick, Kinsale, and Blar-
ney. (Of course, we all kissed the stone.)

The bus was filled with the friendliest and happiest people I had
ever met. There were frequent stops for a "wee bit of refreshment,"
and I realized this was part of a way of life. There must be more
saloons per capita in Ireland than anywhere else in the world. Yet
in the four days we spent in Ireland I never saw anyone intoxi-
cated.

The orchestra had been brought to Ireland through the efforts
of Michael Kelleher, the first Irish-American trustee of the Boston
Symphony Orchestra. At the concert's intermission, Kelleher

Beating Time

made a speech expressing his pride in bringing the Boston Symphony Orchestra to his ancestral city. Mike became so emotional in front of all his relatives (and there must have been a thousand Kellehers in the audience) that he broke down in tears.

The concert was a great success. We were the first American orchestra to play there, although the County Cork Musical Society had brought in many European orchestras, including the Vienna Philharmonic, the Berlin Philharmonic, the London Symphony, and the Leningrad Philharmonic.

As I walked through the streets of Cork the next day, I was particularly intrigued by a sign on a shop window, "Hyman Nathan, Tailor." I couldn't resist going in. An old man greeted me. "Are you Hyman Nathan?" I asked.

"That I am," he answered in a thick brogue. When I told him I was with the Boston Symphony, he exclaimed, "The blessings o' God upon ye! Sit down. I came to your concert last night." Like most Irishmen he seemed to have plenty of time for talking, so we passed a very pleasant half hour. When I asked him if he had been born in Ireland, he said, "Oh, no, I was born in Poland. I came here as a young man." He had been an itinerant peddler, traveling all throughout Europe, and had settled in Cork.

"Why Cork?" I asked.

He was silent for a moment, then blurted out, "I'll be goddamned! I never thought about it before." He insisted that I go home to dinner with him to meet his wife and large family of children and grandchildren, but I had to refuse because we were leaving for Dublin. His last words were, "Too bad. Mama makes the best bloody gefilte fish in all of Ireland!"

From Cork we went to Dublin, then gave six concerts in Edinburgh and one each in Copenhagen, Oslo, and Stockholm. A con-

Touring the Continent

cert in Helsinki, Finland, was followed by two in Leningrad and three in Moscow. From Russia we went to Prague and Vienna, then Stuttgart, Munich, Zurich, Bern, and two concerts in Paris. From Paris we went to Chartes, where we played in the magnificent cathedral, then back to Paris to catch a flight to England for a concert at Leeds, and then to London for our final two concerts, arriving back in Boston on September 28. In all, the tour lasted thirty-four days, during which we gave twenty-nine concerts in eighteen cities in thirteen countries. Of our five "rest days," two were in London after we had given our final concert.

We were the first American symphony orchestra ever to play in the Soviet Union, and the excitement among the players and even throughout the United States was high. Before our departure we were briefed on the cultural and diplomatic importance of our visit by a member of the State Department, who advised us on our behavior while in the country. We were asked not to engage in politics, ours or theirs; not to denigrate their system; not to boast of ours; to be as discreet as possible in our conversation with the Soviets; and to remember at all times that we were guests of their government. We were also asked not to photograph planes, airports, or bridges.

Our last concert before entering the Soviet Union took place in Helsinki, Finland. The next morning we assembled at the airport in Helsinki and were told that we would be flown to Leningrad in small Russian planes, each taking about thirty passengers. Before takeoff I surreptitiously aimed my camera out of an airport window and took a picture of the first Russian plane I had ever seen. Any minute I expected to be apprehended, but nobody saw me.

After we boarded our plane I fumbled for my seat belt, which,

Beating Time

I discovered, had only one strap. I called the stewardess. "Oh," she said, "don't worry. It will be a smooth flight. Not necessary, seat belts!" Then I asked her if I could smoke. "Why not?" she said. "Pilot is smoking." Just then the copilot jumped into the plane and pulled the door shut, and before he made it to the cockpit, we were already moving. It was the quickest takeoff I had ever seen. We taxied to the end of the runway, turned without stopping, and in about ten seconds were airborne. The flight from Helsinki to Leningrad, over the Gulf of Finland, took about an hour. Our descent to the Leningrad airport was even more hair-raising than our takeoff. There was no gradual descent. The plane seemed to plummet from the sky to the ground. After a quick taxi to the terminal, the copilot ran from the cockpit before the plane had come to a stop, and opened the door.

We were met by a rather large delegation from the Ministry of Culture, plus a few musicians from the Leningrad Philharmonic Orchestra, with flowers and extremely friendly greetings. We had to wait for the other planes to arrive before there was an official greeting. Meanwhile we made small talk, in English with those who understood, and through an interpreter with others. One lady from the delegation said, "I notice you have cameras. Why don't you take pictures?" We told her we had been advised not to take pictures of airports or planes. "Nonsense!" she said. "Please take all you wish."

Finally, when the other planes arrived and the entire orchestra was assembled on the field, the minister of culture made a welcoming speech in Russian, and her words were translated into English for us. Then we were driven to the Europa Hotel, situated across the street from Philharmonic Hall, where we were to play.

After being assigned to our rooms, we were asked to go to the

Touring the Continent

dining room for breakfast. This was a sumptuous repast that included eggs, caviar, many varieties of smoked fish, black and white bread, butter and cheese, and a hot beverage that was called coffee but bore little resemblance. It was a strange brew of mostly chicory and milk, all cooked together and served in a glass. I think I was the only one who enjoyed it because it reminded me of my mother's "coffee." The restaurant, we were told, was at our disposal any time of day or night, and everything was free except wines and liquors. After breakfast the orchestra was taken on a tour of Leningrad, accompanied by three guides who pointed out with great pride the interesting aspects of their city.

That night, since there was no concert, the orchestra was taken to a Russian theater to see a play. Having other plans, I did not go and was later told that I had missed a very boring evening. No one understood the actors or could follow the plot, but all had to sit through to the bitter end. I, on the other hand, went with Victor Manusevitch, a fellow violinist, to the home of a Russian family: a father, mother, and twenty-year-old son. The father was a professor of philosophy at Leningrad University, the son a student of languages at the same university whose hobby was collecting Louis Armstrong records. He spoke English well enough to act as interpreter. The father had an insatiable desire for information about the United States, and during our conversation, which went on into the early hours of the morning, I realized that I was engaging in just the kind of political talk we were asked to avoid. Yet I couldn't resist. He told me he was not a member of the Communist party, yet he believed that eventually the whole world would become communist, and how could I not agree with him? "But," I said, "what about freedom and personal liberty? Do you really believe that the people of the world want to be enslaved? Do you think the entire world will become a planet of terror, like your country is now?"

"Oh," he answered, "we don't have communism here yet. We have a dictatorship of the proletariat, which is necessary until we can someday have a true communistic society. Up until now we have unfortunately had bad people at the head of our government, but now things will be better."

By that time we had discovered that we could continue the conversation in Yiddish, so we dispensed with the son's translation. Then he asked what we in America thought of Khrushchev. I knew the Russian word *grobyan* (vulgarian) and blurted it out. He looked at his son, then glanced furtively around the room, and said, "I, too!"

Our Leningrad concert coincided with Rosh Hashanah, the Jewish New Year, so a few of us decided to look for a synagogue, which, in spite of many devious answers from officials and attempts at dissuasion by our guides, we found. It was the only Jewish temple in Leningrad and was crowded to the doors. When the elders spied us, they immediately escorted us to the *bimah* (pulpit). After the service, we went outside and were followed by most of the congregation, then plied with questions. "Are there many synagogues in the U.S.?" "Are there any Jews in government?" "Is it true that Roosevelt was really Rosenfeld?" "Was Avram Lincoln a Jew?"

After the last Leningrad concert we went back to the hotel. I was talking to Thomas Perry, our manager, when the minister of culture, a woman, came into the lobby followed by three men, one carrying a paper bag. She approached Perry and asked him to follow her into an anteroom. I went along and was dumbfounded to see one of the men empty the contents of the paper bag on a

Touring the Continent

table. Thousands of rubles poured out! This, Perry was told, was our fee for the concerts. He stuffed the money back into the paper bag and thanked the minister. The next day we were given hundreds of rubles to spend as we pleased. Since it was forbidden to take any of it out of the country, there was a mad dash for the department stores. I still have a black fur hat and six silver teaglass holders.

After the last concert in Leningrad, we left for Moscow by night train. Most of us preferred to stay up all night rather than use the bunk beds (there were four in each compartment). Fortunately, there was a dining car, where we spent the night playing cards and playfully teasing the buxom female attendants. Such was the strict puritanism of the Russians then that when one of my colleagues dared to pinch the cheek of one of the attendants, there was almost an international scandal. The conductor was called, and if one of our Russian colleagues had not explained the innocence of the gesture, we might all have been arrested.

On our arrival in Moscow we were taken to the newest hotel, the Peking, which was so new that nothing worked. The tiny elevators in this "modern" hotel accommodated only three people. The dining room was not yet open, so we had to take all our meals at the Metropole Hotel, a couple of miles away, for which buses were provided. The rooms themselves were reminiscent of the gay nineties, with their heavy red-draped windows and enormous four-poster beds. The private bathrooms, a real luxury we were told, were the size of telephone booths, and the new tiles on the floor were inexpertly laid. The water barely trickled except in the middle of the night, when it would suddenly burst forth, unbidden.

There seemed to be a pervasive fear of contact with the outside

Beating Time

world among the Russian people. Victor Manusevitch, a violinist who left his native Russia to study in Germany and then came directly to America without returning to his homeland, had expressed the fear that if he returned to the Soviet Union he might not be able to come back to the United States. Inquiries were made through the orchestra management to the U.S. State Department, and Victor was assured that there would be no problem. He had a brother in Moscow whom he had not seen for twenty years. In all the time we were in Russia, Victor tried to contact his brother, without success. Then, early in the morning of our last day in Moscow, the telephone rang in our room. Victor answered it and turned white. His brother was in the lobby. He came up to the room and I witnessed a very emotional reunion. Victor's brother later took him to meet his nieces and nephews, but with the warning that he was not to identify himself as their uncle.

One evening we were sitting in the dining room, having just finished a midnight snack, when our guide, a rather attractive young woman who spoke English perfectly, asked us if we would like to see the new Moscow subway. A number of us went along even though we were exhausted. The trains were immaculate and the stations had beautiful murals, all depicting some phase of the revolution. We rode to the outskirts of Moscow, and at precisely 1:00 A.M. the train came to a halt at the last station, where the conductor announced something. Our guide translated, "End of the line," then informed us that all trains stop at that hour. We were escorted back by taxis, which mysteriously appeared when we emerged into the street.

Our concerts in Leningrad and Moscow were successes, with people surrounding us after each concert and either staring or say-

Touring the Continent

ing some words in English, occasionally asking if we knew a relative in Chicago. One man approached me after a concert in Moscow and asked if I knew his cousins, Phil and Leopold Spitalny. (Phil Spitalny was then well known in the U.S. as the conductor of his All-Girl Orchestra; his brother, Leopold, was the manager of the NBC Symphony.) A theater conductor, he had not been in touch with his cousins for years, and when I offered to send them his greetings he agreed, but added, "Please ask them not to write to me."

After our last concert in Russia we were tendered a state banquet in the Metropole Hotel. This was a gala affair with lots of borscht and vodka and many speeches. Dmitri Kabalevsky, who spoke English quite well, was the toastmaster, and he called on many of his colleagues for speeches, among them Dmitri Shostakovich, Aram Khachaturian, David Oistrakh, Mstislav Rostropovich, Leonid Kogan, Kirill Kondrashin, and many others. I remember particularly the words of Khachaturian: "Today I heard sounds from an orchestra that I never thought possible, and now that I have heard you and what you can do, I must write something especially for you."

That night, or rather the next morning, we began our exodus from Russia—again in shifts. The first group left for the airport at 2:30 A.M., the rest following in one-hour intervals. We were on our way to Prague with a stopover in Vilna. Our plane came down in Vilna at 8:00 A.M., and we were ushered into the airport restaurant for breakfast, which, we discovered, consisted of roast chicken and cucumbers. I asked the waitress if this was the standard breakfast. "Well," she answered, "we never know the time planes arrive. If you arrive at dinnertime you would get the same meal."

Beating Time

Since that 1956 visit, the Soviet Union has passed into history. Other American and European orchestras have toured Russia more recently; conditions there, they say, have improved greatly.

In 1979, some seven years after President Nixon's visit there had improved relations, the Boston Symphony went to China. We were the first orchestra to be invited to China after the establishment of good relations with that country. The Philadelphia Orchestra had played there when the Gang of Four was in power and had received scathing reviews condemning them for playing "decadent" music such as Beethoven and Brahms! Our trip to China was especially exciting for Seiji Ozawa for, although Japanese, he was born in Manchuria and lived as a child in Shanghai, where his father, a dentist, was an officer in the Japanese occupation army.

We were treated most hospitably. There were two concerts in Shanghai and two concerts in Beijing. At our final concert the Beijing Orchestra joined us in Beethoven's Fifth Symphony. I sat next to a Chinese violinist who spoke some English; he seemed happy to be playing Western music, which until recently had been forbidden.

We gained an insight into the appalling conditions under which our Chinese colleagues had tried to make music. Since Western music was prohibited, the musicians had played and practiced surreptitiously, always terrified they would be caught and punished. The concertmaster of the Beijing Orchestra had spent eleven years in prison for publicly advocating Western music. During the intermission he became engaged in a heated discussion with Eugene Lehner, one of our violists; when I came closer, I realized

Touring the Continent

they were speaking in Lehner's native Hungarian. The concert-master had been a student in Budapest.

After our final concert we were taken to the famous Peking Duck restaurant in Beijing, which stayed open for us. By this time we had all learned how to use chopsticks. The chef and his assis-tants, in their white coats and tall hats, paraded before the meal, displaying on trays the beautiful roasted ducks they were to cut and serve. When we left Beijing the next day, crowds of people came to the airport see us off, and to gawk at the first Boeing 747 ever to land in China.

19

Variations on a Theme

Variation I: The Archdiocese of Boston

☞ In the mid-1960s I was asked to take over the training and conducting of the Boston Catholic Youth Orchestra, which I did for about five years. During that time we also formed a nuns' orchestra made up entirely of teaching sisters in the archdiocese of Boston. Both of these orchestras turned out to be interesting experiences for me. To put it generously, the musical abilities of neither the students nor teachers were of high caliber. Yet I was able to find music for them that was playable as well as challenging. We actually gave some concerts. There was a concert in Symphony Hall, attended by the beloved Cardinal Cushing, performed by the youth orchestra, the nuns' orchestra, and the nuns' chorus. I don't remember what or how we played, but there was great enthusiasm from the audience, made up mostly of parents, relatives, and friends. The highlight of the occasion, as I remember it, was a long, rambling speech by the cardinal. (Some time later, at a function in Temple Ohabei Shalom, I met him. "Aren't you one of *my* employees?" he asked.)

My Orthodox Jewish mother's reaction to my association with

Beating Time

Catholics was ambivalent, but typical of her innate broadmindedness. At one of my Boston Pops concerts she was visiting me during intermission when in walked my good friend Monsignor Christopher Griffin. He was not wearing his priestly collar. "Is this your mother, Harry?" he asked, kissing her on the cheek. I am quite sure my mother had never been kissed by a priest before, and when Msgr. Griffin left I said, "Mama, do you know who that was?" "A nice young man," she answered. When I told her he was a priest, her comment was: "My son, they are good people too."

Once, when she saw my picture in the newspaper with a group of nuns, she called me and asked: "What are you doing with all those sisters?" When I told her that I was conducting their orchestra, she asked, "Do they pay you?" "Yes, Mama," I said. She replied, laughingly, "Then it's all right." Actually, her reaction was one of pride. She would boast to her Jewish friends, "The Catholics had to take my son to teach them."

Variation II: A Rehearsal of Modern Music

Conductors are constantly receiving unsolicited scores from composers, and many pile up on shelves unread. Koussevitzky once announced that there would be a special rehearsal for new music, unsolicited compositions that he had hardly had time to look at and which were completely unfamiliar to the players.

This was an evening to remember. We plowed through a number of strange compositions that had very little relationship to music as we knew it. It was bedlam, though Koussey tried to control the proceedings with great seriousness. At one point in the rehearsal our second oboist, Jean Devergie, turned to Fernand Gillet, our first oboist. "What are we playing next?" he asked. Gillet

Variations on a Theme

pointed to the next piece. Devergie exclaimed, "My God! I just played it!"

Variation III: My First (and Last) Appearance with the Met

In the early 1950s one of Boston's landmarks was destroyed. The wonderful old Boston Opera House, on Huntington Avenue between Symphony Hall and the Museum of Fine Arts, was torn down to make room for a parking lot. What a tragic loss! The beautiful hall, well equipped for opera and theater and elegant inside and out, had been the scene of some memorable performances by traveling companies, among them the New York Metropolitan Opera. During one of their visits the opera to be performed was Mozart's *Don Giovanni*, and I, along with a few of my colleagues from the BSO, was engaged to play in the onstage band for the second-act party scene.

We were asked to be at the opera house at 6:00 P.M. for costuming and rehearsal. The Italian costumier was a nervous and temperamental man who looked at us and exclaimed, "Why dey send me giants? I got no costumes for dem!" Indeed, each jacket and pair of pantaloons were much too small for any of us. When I complained that I could not play in such a tight fit he angrily tore off the coat and put it on backward. "Now," he said, "you got more room. And besides, you no play concerto, just a few notes. It'sa good enough." When the trousers would not come together at the waist, he advised, "When you play there is a small fence in front. You just sit very low."

We were given a perfunctory rehearsal by someone who merely

Beating Time

told us to watch the conductor, Bruno Walter. When it came time
to play I tried to find the conductor through the glaring spotlights
and finally made him out, very far away from our perch on the
balcony. After playing a few bars there was a sudden shriek onstage as Zerlina recognized Don Giovanni, and we stopped playing. Next to me was a cellist from the Met orchestra who had
done this scene many times. As soon as we heard the shriek and
stopped playing I saw him throw up his hand and heard him mutter, "Oh, my God!" "What happened?" I asked him. "Nutting," he
answered in his Italian accent, "I'm acting!"

Variation IV: An Attempt to Recreate History

In 1791 Haydn received an honorary degree from Oxford University and conducted his *Oxford* Symphony for the occasion. In 1879
Brahms received an honorary degree from the University of Bres-
lau and conducted his *Academic Festival* Overture. Thus the idea
came to me that the fifteenth anniversary of the establishment of
Brandeis University should be celebrated with music. I made an
appointment with Abram Sacher, then president of Brandeis, and
presented him with the suggestion that the university bestow honorary degrees upon three great soloists of our time, Jascha Heifetz,
Artur Rubinstein, and Gregor Piatigorsky. I also suggested that
they perform Beethoven's Triple Concerto with the Boston Symphony at a celebratory commencement concert in Symphony
Hall.

Dr. Sacher agreed with the idea, although the university had
never given three honorary degrees in the same category. He told
me that if I could arrange it with the three soloists and the BSO
he would go along with it.

Variations on a Theme

Letters signed by Charles Munch were sent to Heifetz, Rubinstein, and Piatigorsky, and we awaited their responses. The first to answer was Piatigorsky, excited and pleased by the prospect. For a long time nothing was heard from the other two, until I met Rubinstein at a concert in New York. He informed me that he wouldn't be caught dead on the same stage with Heifetz. A short while later, a letter came from Heifetz saying he was too busy.

Variation V: The Boston Classical Orchestra

In 1983 I was asked to assume the conducting of a chamber group with a rather odd name, the Boston Classical Orchestra. "Classical?" I wondered, until I learned that the board of trustees was unashamedly averse to modern music. In my ten-plus years of conducting this small orchestra, I have occasionally slipped into the program a piece by Copland or Bartók, but that is about as modern as we go. We give ten concerts a year in the historic Faneuil Hall in Boston, in which many patriotic and political figures have appeared. About the same size as a concert hall in Mozart's time, it is ideal for chamber music. Although we dress formally, I try to make these concerts intimate and informal, even occasionally repeating movements.

Variation VI: Sherm Feller

Until his recent death, Sherm Feller was the voice of the Boston Red Sox. It was he who announced the lineups and made witty remarks over the loudspeaker at Fenway Park.

He was also my friend. Sherm was the zaniest character I ever knew. He had no calling. He had no real job. He had no formal

Beating Time

training, except that he had attended law school, according to him, but never graduated. During the years I knew him, he was for a while a radio talkmaster, songwriter, baseball announcer, and general merchant of things legal and otherwise. He had close friends in all walks of life, doctors, lawyers, politicians, schoolteachers, sports and entertainment figures, prostitutes, thieves, ex-cons.

Sherm was a do-gooder with a big heart, to whom everyone came for help. He was generous to a fault not only with his own money but also with others'. He borrowed a lot, and paid back in kindness. He would suddenly appear at my door laden with food, advising me to put it away quickly. "Where did you get this?" I would ask, savoring the aroma of corned beef or lobster. "I stole it," he would say.

Sherm owed me some money when he died, money which I never expected or wanted to get back. But from time to time he would say, "I know exactly how much I owe you," and would name a figure much below what he had borrowed. He had made periodic repayments with checks that bounced.

I miss him very much.

20

My Family

Mother

∽ My mother's pride in me, her only son, was complete, fierce, and unrestricted. Whenever I left town, even for a few days, she would expect a letter from me—in Yiddish. Over the years she collected a sizable number of them, which she proudly exhibited to all her friends. The Yiddish I learned to read and write was the result of my being tutored as a child by a *milamid* who came to the house five times a week. The *milamid* also prepared me for my bar mitzvah by teaching me to read the Haftarah in Hebrew, which I dutifully chanted without understanding a word. Hebrew was considered a dead language at the time, long before the establishment of the state of Israel, and my parents insisted I learn the more practical language of Yiddish.

My mother's belief in me was pure and obsessive. On October 17, 1969, Temple Ohabei Shalom Brotherhood in Brookline, Massachusetts, gave a Man of the Year dinner for me. It was a memorable affair, and at the head table with me, in addition to the officers of the brotherhood and a number of trustees of the Boston Symphony Orchestra, were Arthur Fiedler and other dignitaries. There were the usual speeches, followed by a short concert played by

Beating Time

my friend and colleague Joseph Silverstein, the concertmaster of the BSO. In the audience were my wife, my children, and my mother. At the end of the ceremonies I said a few words. "I'm honored and most grateful and quite embarrassed, for I know there are people in this audience who deserve this honor more than I. However, there is one person here who knows I deserve it. When I told my mother, 'They're having this evening just for me,' she unhesitatingly said, 'Why not?'"

All my life I was her "little boy." When she was in her middle eighties she decided to visit a cousin in New Jersey. I was in New York with the orchestra at the time and arranged to meet her in Penn Station. She arrived carrying two valises. When I tried to take them from her, she said, "Take the little one, the big one is too heavy for you."

My mother was a no-nonsense pessimist. One always had to be careful about tomorrow while making the best of today. Once she was being examined for eyeglasses, and when asked by the doctor how well she could see, she said, "Not so good, but what is there so good to see in life?" At one session she almost drove the doctor to distraction when she wouldn't read the eye chart. "The big letter anyone can see," she said. "The next line is good too, but after that it's blurry."

"Please, Mrs. Dickson, read me the letters," the doctor pleaded.

"Why should I read you the letters? You know what they are."

"Yes, Mrs. Dickson, but I can't tell if *you* know what they are."

"Doctor," she answered, "do you think I would fool you?"

Jane

My forty-two-year marriage to Jane ended when she died of cancer in December 1977. Our marriage was a strange one. Of course

My Family

we loved each other; as the years went by she was my anchor, my protector, my nurturer, my life. Yet I really never knew her. There was always a side of her I did not know. She was the most private human being I have ever known, and there were aspects of her thinking, her past life, her real self that were never revealed. And I never asked.

Jane's background was unusual. Her father was Irish, her mother a Hungarian Jew. She was adopted as an infant by Mabel and Henry Goldberg, a childless couple of ample financial means who lived in New Rochelle, New York. The Goldbergs were a completely mismatched couple and later divorced. Henry was a Southerner from Nashville, Tennessee, a right-wing conservative, charming, debonair, but basically narrow and prejudiced. Mabel, on the other hand, was a left-leaning liberal.

Shortly after I first met Jane in Berlin in 1931, I learned she had been adopted. Everyone seemed to know it. It wasn't until years later that I discovered the strange saga of Jane's life. Why was she adopted? Why did her natural mother give her up? For a long time I believed that Jane's biological parents had been married and that her father had died. The truth was that they were prevented from marrying by religious pressure from both of their families. Through the efforts of Rabbi Stephen Wise, Jane was adopted by the Goldbergs. The terms of the adoption were that Jane's mother, Margaret, was to live with the Goldbergs as governess. Jane did not find out that Margaret was her own mother until her eighth birthday. It was a year later that Mabel Goldberg made her decision that "children should have a European education" and took Jane off to be educated in France and later in Germany, where she would visit Jane occasionally.

Margaret later married and had three children, none of whom had the slightest inkling of their relationship to Jane. Some years

Beating Time

later Bob, the elder son, came to Boston to study at Boston University and, of course, lived with us. One evening when I was at a concert Jane took him for a walk and abruptly informed him that she was his half sister. The astonished Bob could only mutter, "You mean Kitty and Jinny are my nieces?"

On occasional Boston Symphony trips to New York, when school was out, Jane and the children would come with me for the four- or five-day stay. While Jane stayed with me in the hotel, the children stayed with "Aunt Margaret," her family never guessing the relationship. No one seemed to notice the family resemblance of Jane to Margaret's children, nor the tear in Margaret's eye when she warmly smothered her grandchildren in hugs and kisses.

Neither of my own daughters knew that "Aunt Margaret" was really their grandmother. They did not find this out until much later when, in their teens, a relative of Jane's spoke of their mother's adoption. Stunned and confused, they asked their mother, "Why didn't you tell us?" Jane's answer was typically evasive: "Now you know."

Jane was fanatic about privacy. Her most painful moments were when she had to appear in public. When she came with the children to one of my concerts, she would never applaud, for fear of attracting attention to herself, and she even admonished the girls. "You don't applaud your own father," she used to say. Jane was terribly uncomfortable when she had to appear with the family at the State House to witness the inauguration of her son-in-law Michael Dukakis as governor of Massachusetts. She had an abhorrence of politics and would call Mike from time to time urging him to resign. She adored him and often told him, "You're too good for this."

During World War II Jane felt a compulsion to do her patriotic

My Family

duty. She volunteered to work nights at Raytheon, a defense contractor. The routine was bizarre. I would return from a concert at about 10:30 P.M., in time for Jane to leave. She would return at 7:30 A.M., serve us breakfast, get the girls off to school, then go to bed. This went on every day for about a year.

Even Jane's dying was done in her way: regally and properly. When she found out she had cancer, she discussed her options with the physician and accepted them calmly and quietly. I drove her to the hospital for periodic chemotherapy treatments. On our return she would seek the privacy of the bedroom, only to emerge two hours later to prepare dinner as usual.

When she was finally hospitalized, it was with the understanding that she would come home to die. The day after Jane came home from the hospital, she asked me to go for a walk with her. The nurse who had been assigned to be with her at home objected, but Jane insisted. "If you go for a walk," the nurse said, "I'll leave." "Fine," was Jane's reply, "good-bye." Despite her debilitating illness, Jane insisted on running the household. I still have a vision of her coming downstairs every morning until the end to prepare breakfast. I would urge her to eat, not realizing that she was actually starving herself.

Although Jane has been gone nearly twenty years, we were recently reminded of her private ways. Ever since Jane died, the girls had been wondering what had happened to their mother's silver, which she had inherited but never used. I received a call one day from "Putt" Darey, the genial caretaker of our summer place at Tyringham, in the Berkshires. "I found the loot," he informed me. She had carefully wrapped the silver in six cloth bags and stashed it away in the attic of the guest house.

Even in dying, Jane's greatest concern was for me. "How will he

Beating Time

get along?" she voiced her fear to the children, and exacted from them a promise to care for me. The years have gone by, and she needn't have worried. I am now blessed with the love and concern of my daughters, their husbands, nine grandchildren, and three great-grandchildren, and I am rarely alone.

"Grammy": Jane's Mother

Mabel Goldberg, Jane's adoptive mother, was a character, a kook, an inveterate do-gooder, a fiercely independent free-thinker, a well-read intellectual, a selfless human being who cared not one whit what others thought of her. She was totally devoid of humor and had an inner drive to right all the wrongs of this world. She had a nervous tic and chain-smoked unfiltered cigarettes, which for some reason she would cut in half before smoking both ends down to the butt. At the age of sixty-five Mabel went back to Columbia University for her Ph.D. in social work, and although she never used her degree, it became part of her personality. She decided what was right for us and proceeded to act on her decisions. She never seemed to sleep. The light was on most of the night in her room while she read and smoked. One night, about three in the morning, she knocked on the bedroom door of our summer cottage on Cape Cod, where she had been staying with us.

"Children, are you awake?" she asked.

"We are now," I answered.

"Do you have any charge accounts?" she wanted to know. She was absolutely opposed to the use of charge accounts. "If you can't afford it, you shouldn't buy it" was her motto.

"Yes," Jane answered.

My Family

"How much do you owe?"

It took a few minutes for Jane and me to figure it out in our heads, but we came up with a figure of $850.

"If I give you the money, will you promise never to charge things again?" she asked.

We nodded and she left the room. In the morning I asked Jane, "Did you dream something about Mother coming into our room in the middle of the night? Well, it was no dream. Here's eight hundred and fifty dollars she left on the dresser."

Once while I was in New York with the orchestra, I met her at Grand Central Station. She had come in from New Rochelle to attend our afternoon concert in Carnegie Hall, and as we walked from the station, we passed the Emigrant Savings Bank on 42nd Street. "Do you have a good violin?" she asked me. I told her it was so-so. "Well, I think you should have a good one. I think I have an account in this bank." We went in, and ten minutes later I walked out with a check for five thousand dollars. In those days that was a sizable amount, and I was able to buy a beautiful Guadagnini.

During the war Grammy lived in Lexington, Massachusetts. One day our front doorbell rang and a man said, "Harry Dickson? I have a car for you." I was incredulous, but the man insisted and offered to drive back to the garage so he could demonstrate it to me. She had bought us a car—a brand-new Kaiser-Frazer—so that we could visit her in Lexington. That was Grammy!

My Girls, Kitty and Jinny

My daughters have always been close to me. They are quite different in their personalities. Kitty, the older by fifteen months, has

Beating Time

always been the more sensitive, the more fragile one, the one most easily hurt. Jinny is the rock of our family, ready at all times to give of herself, to protect and nurture her sister. She is also the renegade, given to making shocking remarks. When they were in their early teens we were sitting at dinner one night and the conversation turned to boys and dating. "Look here, girls," I said, "you're not the ugliest in the world and I suppose you'll be going out with boys. Please remember, if you ever get into any kind of trouble, you come to me."

"Of course," said Jinny, "who else would pay for it?" Their mother was shocked.

In our family it was I who educated the children about sex. Whenever they came to me with questions, I always answered them truthfully, never trying to lecture them or telling them more than they asked. Their devoted mother, constantly concerned about the rightness of things, never could bring herself to answer their questions. "Ask Daddy," she would say. Indeed, Jinny later said to me, "Why did you tell us all that stuff? It would have been fun to hear it from our girlfriends!" I knew she was pulling my leg.

There have been unpredictable happenings in our lives. Who could have foreseen that Kitty would one day be the First Lady of Massachusetts, or the wife of a presidential candidate? Or a substance abuser? (I still wince when she refers to herself as an "alcoholic.") Who could have foreseen the price she would have to pay for being in the limelight, for never losing her vulnerability, her sensitivity, her concern for others. Indeed, her caring for others has caused her pain and thus spurred Kitty to action throughout her life. In the third grade she brought home from school one day a cross-eyed little boy whom she had befriended because others made fun of him. When one of her neighbors died and the family was in dire circumstances, it was Kitty who established, with the

My Family

help of all her friends and neighbors, a fund for the widow and family, administered anonymously through a bank. It was Kitty who went to Thailand, met the queen, and was able to rescue two Cambodian refugees, one of whom later graduated from Harvard, the other from Brown.

Kitty is remarkable in many ways. Basically lacking in self-confidence, she nevertheless has been able to gather the strength to fight her addiction successfully.

Jinny, who describes herself as "the other one," is equally re-markable. While she stood back and allowed her sister to stand in the spotlight, she has done so with pride and satisfaction. Jinny possesses an innate understanding and compassion for other people's problems and a desire to help and nurture. For twenty years she was a kindergarten teacher, beloved by her students.

Jinny's husband, Al Peters, is an outgoing and personable human being. With Al, nothing is in moderation. When he took up skiing he did it with a vengeance—two hundred days a year. A retired dentist who practiced for forty years in perhaps the busiest office in Boston, Al now travels regularly to Central America to bring dental care to the poor. A recovering alcoholic—fifteen years sober—Al has been instrumental in having his professional peers recognize and take steps to treat substance abuse among dentists. Al is a charter member of the American Dental Association's Committee on Chemical Dependency, and he frequently uses his expertise (he has recently added a Master's degree in so-cial work to his medical degree) to help others. A good guy!

Michael Dukakis

When Michael Dukakis married Kitty, he became an integral part of my life. Jane, who referred to him as "The Saint," used to com-

Beating Time

pare him with me, and I invariably came out on the bottom. Mike is an incurable optimist, and even in one of the lowest periods of his life, when he lost the presidential election, he still had a sense of awe at having come so far. He is the simplest of men, eschewing all pomp and ceremony, satisfied with what simply meets his needs. I would guess that he is the only governor of Massachusetts who commuted to the State House on the streetcar. He does his own marketing, his own shopping, and his own gardening, and occasionally cooks for the family. He does all of this not for effect, not to impress anyone, but because of his innate simplicity. During the presidential campaign he was irritated by being surrounded constantly with Secret Service agents, whom he tried to ignore. It was a strange sight indeed to see the governor of Massachusetts and candidate for president of the United States scurrying up and down the aisle of the supermarket, three Secret Service men trailing behind. I knew he had a strong sense of ethics when I facetiously called him once to tell him I had received a parking ticket. His reply was, "You've got twenty-one days to pay it." As a student at Swarthmore—from which, incidentally, he graduated summa cum laude with what were among the highest marks in the history of the school—Mike organized a boycott against barbers who refused to serve black students, and even learned barbering so he could cut their hair himself.

It had never occurred to me that I would one day become involved in a very personal way in politics. When Mike became governor in 1975 I basked in his reflected glory. The morning after his election, Sir Colin Davis was conducting a rehearsal of the BSO. The music was Brahms' Fourth. Davis gave a downbeat and my colleagues played "Happy Days Are Here Again" (very badly). Having a son-in-law in the State House added a new dimension

My Family

to my public appearances. I was not only a member of the Boston Symphony Orchestra, not only the associate conductor of the Boston Pops, but also the governor's father-in-law. But as I used to say, I had my job long before he had his. Mike Dukakis served three terms as governor of Massachusetts, more than any other man in the more than 350-year history of the commonwealth.

The presidential campaign consumed me and my family. Even though my inbred pessimism would not allow me even to accept the possibility that Mike could be president of the United States, I willingly let myself be drawn into the fun of campaigning throughout the country. And when the polls began to rise in Mike's favor, I began to doubt my own pessimism.

I don't know what effect I had on the campaign, but I do know that it was fun for me. I was assigned with Mike's mother, Euterpe, mostly to senior citizens' groups throughout the country, and was given position papers on Mike's concern for the elderly, which I never read. I would tell the audience that I was a musician, not a politician, and that half of my fellow musicians in the Boston Symphony Orchestra had already been promised cabinet positions. (Our first oboist was going to be the ambassador to Italy.) I talked about the human side of Mike and his concern for others. I also pointed out that Mike's mother was in her middle eighties, I was approaching that, and between his mother and me, we would make sure that we, the senior citizens, would be well taken care of. I can't recall how many banquets I attended, or how many Democratic clubs I addressed, or how many mayors and governors I met. It was a kaleidoscope of events and happenings. At one banquet somewhere in New Jersey, the chairman, Senator Frank Lautenberg, insisted that I conduct their five-piece band, which I did with great gusto and to enthusiastic applause. The senator

Beating Time

proudly and rhetorically announced, "Does George Bush have a father-in-law who can do that?"

The evening of November 8, 1988, was probably the most depressing one in my life. I had gone with Mike and Kitty to publicly concede the election to George Bush. There were crowds of well-wishers, reporters, and cameras. Mike made his speech, then went home to an eerie silence. He sat exhausted, completely spent, while Kitty acted out her role of sympathetic nonchalance.

The next morning, Mike went back to the State House, and Kitty, all alone at home after a year of unbelievable excitement and adulation, sank into a fit of depression. Gone were the Secret Service protectors, gone were the secretaries, gone were the fawners and the well-wishers. The children were off on their various pursuits. She was truly alone. Kitty had had a bout of diet pill addiction some years back, and now her tendency to addiction took over. When Mike returned home that evening he found her in bed in a drunken stupor and very ill. During her entire public life no one had ever seen her drink more than a cocktail at dinner. Mike was beside himself. This was a new and unexpected problem, which he had no way of handling.

Kitty has written her own book, which describes her years of treatment and her new life. There is renewed optimism in the Dukakis family as Mike, now a professor at Northeastern University, and Kitty, a graduate student at Boston University, share an interesting and purposeful life.

21

Before the Curtain Falls: Retirement from the BSO

ᴄᶠ There is no specified retirement age in the Boston Symphony Orchestra. When a player gets along in years, he or she is usually summoned to the manager's office for a pleasant conference. During the season of 1986 Tom Morris, the manager, called me into his office—and I knew why. This was my forty-eighth year with the orchestra. I had passed my seventy-seventh birthday. Didn't I think it was time to consider putting the fiddle away? Although I half expected it, I was still shocked by the reality, and told Tom I would talk to Ozawa about it. The next day I went to see Seiji. He was, as usual, very warm, very friendly.

"Seiji," I asked him, "do you think it's time for me to leave the orchestra?" Like most Orientals, Seiji has an innate respect for older people. I knew he would find it hard to be truthful without offending me. "You're strong, you're a good player, but I think you lose concentration," he said. I wasn't sure what he meant except that he must have felt that anyone my age must lose interest in

Beating Time

merely playing in an orchestra. "But you can't leave the orchestra altogether," he continued. "You're an institution in Boston! You must continue to conduct the Pops and your youth concerts. You will always be a part of the Boston Symphony!"

Frankly, it had been my expressed desire to round out fifty years as a member of the orchestra. In the history of the BSO the record of longevity was held by Rolland Tapley, a former colleague of mine who had spent an incredible fifty-seven years in the orchestra before retiring. But I said, "Seiji, how about one more year?" to which he readily agreed. My last concert as a player in the BSO took place at the end of the Tanglewood season in August 1987. Now when people ask me why I didn't go another year to fifty, I hide my true feelings by saying, "I'm glad you asked why I didn't, rather than why I did."

On July 26, 1987, a few weeks before my final concert with the BSO, I was given a farewell dinner at the Lenox Club by Fran Fahnestock, one of our favorite trustees of the orchestra. I was "roasted" unmercifully by my colleagues, but I reserved my own remarks for the end. This is what I said:

"The time has now come for me to express my deep appreciation to all my colleagues for their invaluable help and encouragement during all these years. First, to my longtime colleague and friend Leo Panasevich, for never allowing success to go to my head, and for his constant reminder, 'You know you'd be nothing without us!' To my equally valued and distinguished colleague Max Winder, for his honest and expert criticism, 'You have two tempi. Too fast or too slow!' I am also grateful to Matt Ruggiero, who has never criticized me only because he hasn't noticed me. Invariably he has asked in the morning after I have conducted,

Before the Curtain Falls: Retirement from the BSO

'Where were you last night?' A person I have missed very much since his retirement a few years ago is Roger Shermont. Somehow, I never took his caustic remarks very seriously. His words of consolation still ring in my ears, 'You think I'm your worst enemy? Believe me, I'm not.'"

Finale

∽ "To regret the past, never to be satisfied with the present, and to fear the future." That is how Tchaikovsky once described his own life, and I have facetiously said it about myself.

On November 7, 1991, Mayor Raymond Flynn, on behalf of the people of the city of Boston, dedicated a small park close to Symphony Hall in my honor. I am very grateful. My friend Danny Kaye would surely have said, "It looks like you're dead!" I hope to sit in the park from time to time and contemplate my being dead while I am still very much alive and still beating time—before the curtain falls.

Brookline, Massachusetts
January 1, 1995

Index

Index

Index

Index

Index

Index

Index

Index

Index

Index

Index